The Observer's Pocket Series
WILD ANIMALS

Observer's Books

NATURAL HISTORY
Birds · Birds' Eggs · Wild Animals · Zoo Animals
Farm Animals · Freshwater Fishes · Sea Fishes
Tropical Fishes · Butterflies · Larger Moths
Insects and Spiders · Pond Life · Sea and Seashore
Seashells · Dogs · Horses and Ponies · Cats · Pets
Trees · Wild Flowers · Grasses · Mushrooms
Lichens · Cacti · Garden Flowers · Flowering Shrubs
House Plants · Vegetables · Geology · Fossils
Weather · Astronomy

SPORT
Association Football · Cricket · Golf · Coarse Fishing
Fly Fishing · Show Jumping · Motor Sport

TRANSPORT
Automobiles · Aircraft · Commercial Vehicles · Ships
Motorcycles · Steam Locomotives · Small Craft
Manned Spaceflight · Unmanned Spaceflight

ARCHITECTURE
Architecture · Churches · Cathedrals

COLLECTING
Awards and Medals · Coins · Postage Stamps
Glass · Pottery and Porcelain · Firearms

ARTS AND CRAFTS
Music · Painting · Modern Art · Sculpture
Furniture · Sewing

HISTORY AND GENERAL INTEREST
Ancient Britain · Flags · Heraldry · European Costume

TRAVEL
London · Tourist Atlas GB ·
Cotswolds and Shakespeare Country · Lake District

The Observer's Book of
WILD ANIMALS

MAURICE BURTON D.Sc

DESCRIBING 69 SPECIES
WITH 29 COLOUR AND 35
BLACK AND WHITE ILLUSTRATIONS

FREDERICK WARNE
LONDON

Revised edition
© *Frederick Warne & Co. Ltd.*
London, England
1971
Reprinted 1973
Reprinted 1975
Reprinted 1978

ISBN 0 7232 1503 0

Printed in Great Britain by
William Clowes & Sons Limited,
London, Beccles and Colchester
1785.178

PREFACE

Ornithology, the study of birds, has become so popular and widespread during the last half-century as to overshadow the study of other animals. Not surprisingly, there are numerous books about birds and not so many about the rest of the animal kingdom. So far as our native terrestrial vertebrates are concerned, the mammals, reptiles and amphibians, this little pocket volume has helped carry the torch for many years now.

Birds have keen eyesight and colour vision, as we have. They also have a lot to say for themselves, as we are apt to have; and most birds are exhibitionists. The four-legged animals, the quadrupeds or tetrapods, whichever word you prefer, are by nature retiring, fairly silent except at the breeding season, and so tend to make themselves scarce. Even those that make a lot of noise, bats, for instance, do so mainly in the ultrasonic range, beyond the limit of our hearing.

Some of them are scarce, in fact. It seems strange, when one looks back, to realize that twenty years ago you had only to walk down a country road or cross a field to see rabbits. For good or ill—and on the whole it is for good—the rabbit is less common today. As in every other walk in life, change is continuous; one animal becomes rare while another increases in numbers. Otters, always elusive and difficult to observe, are becoming rare, we are told, while the introduced mink has escaped into the wild and is building up in numbers.

Two of the casualties among quadrupeds we must always regret; ironically, we still call them the common frog and the common toad. For a variety of reasons, including the filling in of so many ponds, both are becoming markedly rare, so much so that one gets a thrill now at seeing, outside the breeding season when they congregate in the remaining ponds, a real live specimen of a common frog or a common toad.

On the whole, our quadrupeds are mainly active at night, seen more often in the headlights of a car than by any other means. Even the bold, impertinent grey squirrel has a remarkable capacity for keeping out of sight. The study of our native quadrupeds is, therefore, more arduous than bird watching, but is if anything more rewarding. The sight of a mammal can be something of a collector's piece; to be able to talk about the otter you watched can command respect even in a company of experienced naturalists, most of whom would have to confess to never having seen an otter in the wild.

CONSERVATION OF WILD CREATURES AND WILD PLANTS ACT 1975

This Act makes it illegal, except under licence or in a few other specified circumstances, to kill, injure or take, or to have in your possession any of the following wild creatures:

sand lizard, smooth snake, natterjack toad, greater horse-shoe bat and mouse-eared bat. It is also an offence to sell any of these wild creatures, even if they are dead, including specimens that are in the form of a skin or skeleton.

These protected wild creatures and all species of bat must not be marked or ringed unless a licence has been obtained from the Nature Conservancy Council, 19 Belgrave Square, London, SW1X 8PY.

Copies of the Act are obtainable from HMSO., High Holborn, London, WC1V 6HB.

INTRODUCTION

During the last thirty years or so there has been an almost revolutionary switch towards interest in mammals and also towards the study of reptiles and amphibians. One feature of this is the establishment of two societies: The Mammal Society of the British Isles and the British Herpetological Society. Herpeto is from a Greek word meaning to creep and it is used to signify reptiles, such as the creeping snakes as well as lizards and other less creeping reptiles, and also amphibians, including newts that creep, toads that walk and frogs that jump.

When a new society is formed it is evidence of a growing interest in a particular subject, and I suppose I can say that I have seen the interest grow, especially in mammals. As a boy, I can recall one of the things the average person knew about badgers was that they had a fearsome bite and once they seized anything with their teeth they held on like a bulldog. Another was that badger hams made good eating and badger bristles made good shaving brushes. From time to time one heard about parties of men going out with their dogs and their spades to dig out and kill a family of badgers.

There was another side to the story even then. There were occasionally eccentric people who had a tame badger and there were, perhaps even more occasionally, people who took an interest in the natural history of badgers. What is new today, and has been developing especially over these last thirty-odd years, is the large number of people up and down the country who have spent many nights crouched near the entrance to a badgers' set just for the pleasure of seeing these shy nocturnal animals come out at dusk. There must be many people today who have carried this further and, by patience and persistence, have induced wild badgers to come and eat out of their hands.

Going back again to my youth, I can recall that foxes were notorious because they killed poultry, were crafty, and were referred to as Charley, a reference which, I understand, is to Charles James Fox, a former Prime Minister. In my youth I do not remember anyone saying a good word for Charley or objecting to his being hunted with hounds. Times have changed, and more people now know that not every fox kills chickens or lambs, but that all foxes are the natural enemies of rats and mice.

About thirty years ago one of my neighbours, a widower, had let his large garden run wild after his wife died. He gave me permission to go whenever I chose to do so, to walk among the tussocks of coarse grass, the nettles and the brambles. It was a wonderful place to study natural history, but what I remember most was studying the behaviour of a fox that used often to come to the garden at night. I never saw it actually in the garden, although I several times saw it, just as night was closing in, going towards the hedge surrounding the garden.

I could study the behaviour of the fox by the clues it left: its pawmarks where the ground was soft, the scrapes where it had scratched the soil with its claws, even its droppings helped to build the story, if only as proof that the fox had spent most of the night there. The grass tussocks were ideal shelters for voles and mice, and near them I would find the grass nests dug out, torn apart and thrown to one side. Sometimes, when I dug at one of the scrapes I would unearth, buried lightly beneath the surface, the carcass of a mouse, one the fox had killed when his hunger was satisfied, buried for the future. I could tell these burial spots because a fox scrapes a hole with his forefeet but pushes the earth back with his nose. And he uses his neb to press the earth firmly over his cache.

So I would go round the garden in daylight trying to piece together what the fox had been doing the night before. This particular fox had his earth near a chicken farm, but I never heard of any poultry being killed by it. The evidence I saw in that overgrown garden showed clearly, however, that this fox killed and ate many small rodents. If we think of all the foxes there are in the country and think of all the rats, mice and voles each of them might kill in a year, we begin to understand what the situation might be were all foxes wiped out.

Perhaps this is one of the more interesting features of studying mammals; even if we have difficulty in seeing them, they leave so many traces that we can indulge in gentle sleuthing to fill in the details of their behaviour. It may be true that few people have seen an otter in the wild, but many times that number will have seen their spoor in the mud, remains of their feasts on the river bank, or seen the tracks down a muddy bank where an otter has taken two running steps then slid down on its belly.

After a time, these tracks and signs, together with occasional—or even only exceptional—glimpses of the animal itself begin to build up in your mind until you really feel you know the animal itself intimately. This process is helped enormously today by films broadcast, which supplement so valuably your own observations. To this you can add information by the study of skeletons. For example, it was not until a young friend brought me a badger's skull she had found in the woods that I realized fully how strong is the badger's tenacious grip.

If you found the skull of a rabbit or a fox, as you sometimes can do under the thick layers of dead leaves, in a ditch or under a bank, you may not find any trace of the lower jaw. As the flesh decays the two halves of the lower jaw separate and fall away from the skull. In a badger's skull completely cleaned of its flesh the lower jaw is still in place. Where the two halves engage with the underside of the skull, they are held in a ball and socket joint of the kind you find on some camera tripods. In short, you cannot detach the lower jaw without breaking the bone of the skull. As you hold the skull in one hand and move the lower jaw up and down with the other, you need no words of mine to realize how enormously strong the badger's grip must be.

Should you now find a stoat's skull—and a stoat is a close relative of the badger—you will see that when its lower jaw is raised nearly up to the upper jaw it locks in the same way as the badger's. That is, the arrangement is such that when the stoat's mouth is open the lower jaw, but for the muscles holding it, could drop away from the skull. When it is brought up, as in biting, and just before the teeth meet, it locks as firmly as a badger's. Again, holding a stoat's skull and working the lower jaw up and down, you can see more clearly than any words of mine could tell, just how impossible it would be for a large rabbit to shake off the much smaller stoat, once its teeth had met in the rabbit's neck.

The Mole

Family TALPIDAE   *Talpa europaea*

To those with gardens the work of moles is often
only too evident. From time to time they find that a
tunnel has been driven right across the lawn, spoil-
ing its even surface with an ugly ridge, and at
intervals are little heaps of raw earth. The mole itself
is not so often seen. Its body, highly specialized for
tunnelling, is cylindrical, with no perceptible neck.
The long muzzle is blunt; the eyes and ears are very
small and hidden in the fur. The forelimbs are set
well forward, the hands being relatively large and
broad and wide open—at most they can be only
partially closed—and the palms are always directed
face outwards. The five strong claws serve as efficient picks to supplement the shovel-like palm. The
hindlegs are usually described as weak, but this is
only by comparison with the powerful forelimbs.
They assist in locomotion, especially when the
animal is moving over the surface of the ground, in a
somewhat looping gait, rather like a sea-lion. The
dark grey hairs constituting the velvety fur appear
to be black and are set vertically so that they will lie
forwards or backwards or to either side. This is a
great advantage to an animal needing to move backwards or forwards in a tunnel, or even to turn in its
own width.

Dimensions vary but the males average 14 cm
head and body, the females being slightly smaller.
In both the club-shaped tail, narrow at the base, is
about 32 mm long. The weight is at its maximum
from February to April, and averages nearly 110 g
for a male and nearly 85 g for a female. The young
reach adult size at two to three months.

Colour variations have been recorded; these include normally coloured skins with cream, orange-pink, whitish-black, orange or yellowish markings, as well as skins that are wholly grey, fawn or ash coloured. Albinos have also been found.

It was long ago shown that a mole's eye, although tiny, is complete with lens and retina. There is a good chance that a mole can see stationary objects but that it takes time for the retina to register them. More probably, the mole may use its eyes to detect daylight filtering through the soil, thus enabling it to tunnel just below the surface.

Sight is of less importance to a mole than its sense of smell, but the latter seems to be less acute than was previously supposed. Hearing is acute and there seems to be an ability to appreciate vibrations through the ground. Recently the question has arisen as to whether the mole uses echo-location, based on the scratching sounds of its own claws as it moves underground or, more doubtfully, whether it uses ultrasonics, as bats do. The sounds made when it is chewing or breathing may aid in a kind of general echo-location. It has also been suggested that a mole may know its way around its tunnels by memory based upon its numerous organs of touch. These include thousands of minute papillae on the tip of the snout, sensitive hairs on the tip of the tail and the so-called Pinkus's plates on the skin, especially on the abdomen, in addition to the long whiskers on various parts of the head.

The familiar diagrams of the so-called mole's 'fortress' were the invention of Le Court, the French naturalist. His account, published in 1803, described the interior of the fortress as having a central chamber surrounded by galleries with connecting passages, a central hall, and a bolt-hole communicating with the main run. Plans and elevations were made of these details, and for over a hundred years every writer on the mole reproduced these illustrations without doubting their accuracy. What these writers described as a fortress must not be confused with the 'mole-heaves' thrown up at frequent intervals to get rid of the earth from a newly excavated run. The home of the mole—the molehill proper, containing the nest—is about 30 cm high and about 1 m broad in any direction. As a rule, it will be found partly sheltered by a bush, sometimes well out in a pasture, or it may lie 60 cm underground.

Anyone who has excavated a few dozen molehills

Mole eating an earthworm, holding it down with forepaws

soon learns that they are not constructed to provide a baffling system of bolt-runs for defensive purposes. Their design is incidental to the excavation of the nest cavity and the disposal of the material dug out which often leads to the formation of a solid dome of earth of considerable thickness above it. At certain times of the year, in autumn especially, it is possible to see the molehills not as grass-covered mounds, but as heaps of newly turned soil, standing out among numerous heaves in the fields.

Where moles are established there is an extensive system of runs underground. At about 8–15 cm below the surface is a horizontal system of tunnels forming a square-sided network with more or less vertical shafts to the surface. At about 30 cm below this is a second horizontal system, connected by more or less vertical shafts to the upper horizontal system. From the lower layer of tunnels there are others which run somewhat irregularly downwards, to end blindly 1–1·2 m below the surface. In addition there are the more temporary surface runs. The system of runs described here was observed in sandy soil and no doubt the system will vary in design with the nature of the subsoil.

The male and female (boar and sow respectively) appear to associate only temporarily. The female may mate with several moles (polyandrous). She constructs her own nest-hill, which is said to be smaller and of more simple plan than the male's nest. The hunting tunnels of the female are always said to be winding as compared with the long straight runs of the male. There is, however, little confirmation of this and trapping suggests that both sexes use the same tunnels. The nesting chamber is oval and about 30 cm in longest diameter. The nest itself may be made of grass, leaves or slender twigs, or a mixture of these. The mating season is at the end of March and sometimes in May, and the young are born five to six weeks later. The number of young in a litter varies from two to seven, the usual being three to four. They are blind, naked and pink at birth, but before the fur begins to grow, at about two weeks of age, the skin darkens to a bluish-slate colour. The eyes open on about the twenty-second day. The young leave the nest at about five weeks of age.

The changes in agriculture in these times with reduction of established pastures and hedges, and the use of pesticides, have been detrimental to the mole and may explain the reports in recent years of plagues of moles in certain types of gardens and parks, which presumably act as refuges. Natural enemies include tawny and barn owls, rats, stoats, weasels, foxes, badgers, cats and herons.

The mole's main food is earthworms, but leather-jackets, wireworms and cutworms are also taken, as well as other animal food, dead or alive, when this is available. A mole, like its relatives the shrews, is characterized by a restless activity. Its periods of rest and activity, throughout the twenty-four hours of day and night, appear to be four-hourly. A mole will die of starvation if kept without food for a few hours, which probably accounts for its habit of storing earthworms in considerable numbers.

The mole appears to be plentiful in all parts of England, Wales and Scotland, wherever there are earthworms; it has been found even at a height of 823 m. But it does not occur in Ireland, the Shetlands, Orkneys, Outer Hebrides or the Isle of Man.

The Common Shrew

Family SORICIDAE   *Sorex araneus*

Along the hedge-bank, the ditch-side, or in wood-lands, may be seen one of the smallest and prettiest of our mammals, a minute dusky red-brown creature with long flexible pointed snout constantly turning, testing the air in search of food.

This is the common shrew, inoffensive and useful; its food is restricted to insects, snails and woodlice, together with carrion and a certain amount of grass seed.

With a combined length of head and body amounting to only 57–76 mm, its long hairy tail adds nearly half as much again—but the tail length varies a good deal in different individuals. Its bilobed snout extends far beyond the mouth, and is well furnished with whiskers. The hindfoot—a distin-guishing feature in the shrews—measures just over 12 mm. The weight averages 7·2 g. The shrew has a coat of soft, close, silky fur, dark on the upper part, paling to dirty yellowish grey beneath, and the hairy feet and tail are flesh-coloured. The dark coloration may vary to almost or entirely black. The hairs on the tail are short and stiff. A gland on each flank, midway between elbow and thigh, provides the disagreeable musky odour, the purpose of which is not obvious.

In winter the shrew spends its time in hedge-bottoms and copses among the dead leaves, but not in hibernation. In summer it moves out into the fields and rough pastures, where there are tufts of coarse grass in which it can take cover, and from which it makes runs through the surrounding grass. Here it may be seen at times actually climbing the

Common shrew hunting among yew berries

stout grass stems after insects; sometimes a shrew climbs a tree, up to 3 m in height, presumably in search of food. The toes are well separated, and this enables it to climb. Although the feet are not well formed for digging, it can burrow quickly in light soil with the forefeet, but as a rule it is more inclined to use the underground runs of mice or voles where these are available.

The long, pointed and sensitive snout is well adapted for turning over dead leaves and the surface soil in the search for insects, worms and snails. Its short, velvety fur fits it for passage through the soil without getting dirty.

The nursery is a cup-shaped nest woven of dry grass and other herbage with a loose roof beneath which the shrew makes its entrances and exits. The breeding season extends from May to September in the north, and to October in the south. During this period each female has at least two litters, each consisting of from four to eight or even ten young, the average being just over six. She has only six nipples.

The musky odour makes a shrew actually repellent to some predators but this does not in all cases protect the animal from being killed. Cats, for example, kill many shrews, but will not eat them. Owls, on the other hand, feed largely on them. Other birds of prey, such as the kestrel, are known to take their share, and a considerable number are also claimed by magpies, jackdaws, stoats, vipers and smooth snakes. Where the number of shrews is high, there is a fair chance of casualties through fighting among themselves. There is a general idea that shrews are quarrelsome and always fighting, but in recent years more careful observation of shrews held in captivity, suggests this has been overstated, and injury seldom results from their contests, and when it does it is not severe. When there is overcrowding, however, fighting is more severe.

In all small animals, owing to the great surface area in proportion to the volume of the body, there is a high loss of body heat. Moreover, the smaller the animal, the more quickly it moves. There is, therefore, a proportionately greater need for food to repair the loss of energy, so we find the twenty-four hours of the day and night, in a shrew's life, divided into periods of alternate sleeping and feeding, with peaks of feeding about every three hours. If food is not obtainable for a few hours, the shrew dies.

The common shrew is found throughout Great Britain but not in Ireland. It is also absent from the Scillies, Lundy, Isle of Man, Outer Hebrides, some Inner Hebrides, Orkney and Shetland. Its vertical range is from sea-level to at least 450 m.

The Pygmy Shrew

Family SORICIDAE   *Sorex minutus*

The pygmy or lesser shrew is the smallest of all British mammals. It appears to be widely distributed in Britain, but is local, the areas in which it occurs being limited. These are mostly in wooded districts, but extend from sea-level to the tops of our highest mountains. In Ireland, where it is the only shrew, it is not nearly so abundant as the common shrew is in Britain.

The adult pygmy shrew is only 58 mm long. The hindfoot without the claws in the common shrew is 12 mm, but in the lesser shrew it is one-sixth less. The tail is 38 mm long so is longer in proportion to the body than that of the common shrew. The weight averages 3·5 g with a maximum of 5·6 g.

The colour of the fur is the brown and white of the common species, with a fairly sharp line of demarcation between them. Although the animal as a whole is more delicately built than the common shrew, its snout is relatively longer and thicker, its tail thicker and more hairy, and the forearm and hand shorter. The two types of shrew have much the same habitat yet they seldom mix. Encounters between them are largely avoided because their periods of activity tend not to coincide. During any one day the activity and sleep of a pygmy shrew alternate at closer intervals than those of the common shrew. Moreover, the pygmy shrew shows higher peaks of activity during the day while the higher peaks of the common shrew are during the night.

The pygmy shrew does not appear to construct burrows, but utilizes those of mice or the common

A pygmy shrew

shrew. Its nests have been found in various situations such as a clump of rushes, a hollow tree stump or a hollow in the ground roofed by a stone; and they have been of different materials according to the local conditions, moss, dry grass, fine rush shreds and wood chips variously combined and interwoven to form a hollow ball.

Breeding starts in April, reaches a peak in June and usually ends in August, only rarely going on to October. There are two or more litters a year of from two to eight young.

The Water Shrew

Family SORICIDAE   *Neomys fodiens*

In wandering quietly along the stream side one may see the water shrew on a stone by the margin of the water, for it is active by day as well as by night. Its alternating periods of activity and rest are slightly longer than those of the common shrew. The observer may see it make a sudden plunge into the stream and present a beautiful appearance under water, for the fur carries a good deal of air entangled in it which gives the submerged body a silvery appearance. The water shrew chases the whirligig beetles and water-gnats on the surface, or searches at the bottom for caddis-worms and other larvae. It eats other aquatic animals such as snails, worms, small crustaceans, frogs and small fishes; it is not averse to carrion, and has been caught in a trap baited with cheese. Its bite is said to be poisonous. It utters a cricket-like chirp not unlike that of the other shrews.

The water shrew is frequently seen near a river bank and the quiet observer may then take full stock of its activities, for the limited range of its vision does not permit it to see you. It appears to be very buoyant in the water, swimming with its head slightly above the surface and the body spread out, but it also appears able to walk for a time along the bottom. At times it makes distinct leaps out of the water, apparently chasing a flying insect.

The water shrew is larger and has a finer, more dense fur than the other British species of shrew. The length of head and body combined is 76–96 mm; the body is bulky and the tail longer than the body. The upper parts are slaty black to dark brown, the light ashy grey or dirty white of the underparts appearing pure white by contrast. The snout is short and broad; the small eyes are blue, and the ears, which are entirely concealed, bear a tuft of white hairs. The brown feet are broad and the digits are bordered with stiff hairs which make them very efficient as paddles. The tapering, flattened tail of the adult has a double fringe of strong silver-grey hairs along its underside, constituting a 'keel' and making it more efficient as a rudder. The hind foot usually exceeds 19 mm. Weight is about 12–18 g in adults, and is lowest in winter.

Water shrews burrow into the banks and, far inside, the female lines a chamber with moss and fine roots, or weaves a round nest of grass and leaves where any time from mid-April to September she brings forth her litter of five to eight minute blind

Water shrew swimming

and naked young, the peak being May or June. These develop rapidly and are independent when five or six weeks old. There is probably a second brood in September.

It does not hibernate, and may be seen in winter pursuing its prey beneath the ice. Its chief enemies are owls but it is probably also taken by predatory mammals and fishes.

Sometimes the water shrew is encountered miles from the nearest river or lake, and it is not yet known whether these are resident in such places or whether their presence is fleeting.

The water shrew is much more local in its occurrence than are the other shrews. With this reservation it may be said to be widely distributed throughout England, Wales and Scotland; in Staffordshire and Cheshire it has been found at heights of 300 m. It is not found either in Ireland, the Isle of Man, the Outer Hebrides, the Orkneys or Shetlands.

The Hedgehog

Family ERINACEIDAE   *Erinaceus europaeus*

The hedgehog, urchin or hedgepig is distinct from every other British mammal. Its most characteristic feature is the coat of spines, which are modified hairs. There are other peculiarities, such as the extreme shortness of the head and neck in comparison with the bulk of the body, and the muscular power that enables it to remain rolled into a ball with every part protected by erected spines. The hedgehog is nocturnal, coming out at dusk and hunting through the night. On occasion, it may be seen abroad in full daylight, after a heavy summer downpour of rain has brought out the snails and slugs. These, with insects and worms, constitute the normal diet, but mice, rats, frogs, lizards and snakes are also taken. Some vegetable matter, such as acorns and berries, is eaten and, in captivity, at least some hedgehogs will eat fruit such as apple and pear.

A strange and, until recent years, little-known habit of hedgehogs is that of self-anointing. The animal meeting a substance such as a cigar end, shoe polish, a piece of wood and so on, for the first time, will lick it repeatedly while its mouth becomes filled with a frothy saliva. When the mouth is full of foam, the hedgehog raises itself on its front legs and throws the head to one side, placing flecks of foam on the spines with its tongue. It may then repeat this on the other side; and the process may go on for a long time. There is, as yet, no satisfactory explanation for this remarkable behaviour.

The hedgehog sleeps by day, partially rolled up under a heap of dead leaves or moss. It is often said that one may be guided to a hedgehog's sleeping quarters by its snoring. Few people, however, seem to have actually heard this and the noise may be only the snorts a hedgehog makes when disturbed, as often as not rocking the body slowly from side to side at the same time. Another vocalisation, only heard rarely, is a loud screaming, when the animal is hurt. The usual sound is a quiet grunt, while the young ones give a metallic whistle, almost bird-like.

Hibernation covers the period from October to late March or April. Some individuals sleep through the whole period but in others sleep is intermittent until December or even later. The hibernaculum may be a hole in a bank, but more commonly it is the cavity between the buttress roots of a well-grown tree or under a compost heap. This is lined with dry leaves and moss, carried in by the mouth. During hibernation the body is nourished by fat accumulated during the summer, but the energy requirements are low, for the temperature of the body drops, breathing is so slight that it can hardly be detected and the pulse-rate drops considerably. Also within the body is a dark brown gland known as the hibernating gland or brown fat. This, mainly round the neck and shoulders, is also found in baby mammals and in some adults such as bats and rats. This brown fat is made up of cells containing several droplets of fat. The cells produce heat very quickly and their heat production increases

Hedgehog under a crabtree

rapidly as the temperature of the surrounding air drops, so the fat acts like a thermostatically controlled electric blanket. This prevents the hedgehog from dying of cold should there be a sharp drop in temperature. It is also the brown fat which wakes the animal up at the end of the winter and warms it, so that it quickly becomes active once more.

The hedgehog's eyesight appears to be poor, but its senses of smell and hearing are acute. Hedgehogs have often been condemned for taking hens' eggs and those of wild birds, including partridges and pheasants. This is undoubtedly true, but eating eggs seems not to be a general habit. Another strong belief is that a hedgehog will take milk from a cow. This has often been pooh-poohed but recent evidence, especially of damage to cows' teats, suggests it is true.

A hedgehog is a good swimmer and climber, not

only of trees but of drainpipes and rough walls, especially where these are creeper-clad. There is more than one account of a fight between a rat and a hedgehog in the ivy growing on a wall with the two contestants seeming to be very evenly matched. A hedgehog is also a match for a viper, against whose poison it is immune. Foxes and badgers appear to be the principal enemies.

The male and female are known respectively as the boar and sow. The peak of the breeding season is between May and July, but there may be second litters during August or September. Litters consist of three to seven blind, deaf and helpless young, sparsely clad with pale flexible spines, and with the ears drooping. Between thirty-six and sixty hours after birth a second coat of darker spines begins to appear between the spines of the first coat. The ability to roll up does not come until the young are eleven days old and three days later the eyes begin to open and a third set of spines, ringed with three bands, the middle one dark, the other two lighter in colour, begins to grow out. These are the mature spines, and the first two sets are shed after these have appeared. By this time the baby is a month old, it has started to make excursions from the nest, and is being weaned. Growth is rapid and the young reach sexual maturity the following year.

The adult male hedgehog is up to 26 cm head and body, and the tail is a little over 25 mm; the female is less than the male by about 13 mm. In relation to its entire bulk—its weight being up to 1·2 kg—the neck and body are said to be shorter than in any other British mammal. Both hand and foot have five clawed toes, and five pads on the sole. The legs are very short.

The sharply pointed spines are about 18 mm in length, arranged in radiating groups, surrounded by coarse, harsh fur. Normally the spines lie flat upon the body, but are erected in response to an alarm. They cover the entire upper surface with the exception of the short, conical head and stumpy tail. The spines are quite hard and set almost at right angles to the base so that a hedgehog can fall from a good height unharmed, the spines taking the force of the impact with the ground. The head and underside are clothed with harsh fur of a dirty brown or dirty white colour.

When attacked, a hedgehog has been known to use the skunk-like habit of emitting a highly objectionable odour, but this does not seem to be a general practice.

The Bats
Order CHIROPTERA

With the exception of birds, bats are the only surviving animals that use true flight. The fingers of each hand have been so drawn out that they are longer than the forearm, and the middle finger is at least equal in length to the heady and body, whilst the thumb has been converted into a hook by which the bat can hang from any rough surface. Over these elongated finger-bones stretches a broad web of skin, connected not only to the sides of the body but also to the hindlegs as far as the ankle, and then nearly or quite to the tip of the slender tail. The effect of this is to render the hindlimbs unfitted for ordinary locomotion. They can be rotated until when the bat is crawling over a hard surface, the knee is turned backwards. Some bats at least can land on the ground and take off again or they may run over the ground using the half-folded wings as forelimbs. Bats that roost in roof spaces will run over the rafters or over the vertical faces of walls.

In most bats there is considerable development of the ear as compared with other mammals. The little lobe that guards the entrance to the human ear, known as the tragus, is much elongated so that it becomes a conspicuous feature, and its variation affords one of the characters for the identification of species. Our two horseshoe bats alone are without any prominent tragus.

In flight, a bat's manoeuvrability is superior even to that of birds, especially in the rapidity with which it can change speed, suddenly stopping when in full flight, then making sudden swoops and turning somersaults.

Bats are able to avoid solid objects and catch insects by the use of echo-location. In this, ultrasonic pulses are emitted and the echoes reflected from objects are picked up by the sensitive ears. In most bats the pulses are emitted through the mouth but the horseshoe bats emit them through the nostrils and the nose-leaves, whose characteristic shape gives them their name. These nose-leaves are constantly in motion, concentrating each pulse into a narrow beam that sweeps from side to side.

British bats are all nocturnal in their habits, although a few indulge in occasional flights by day. Most of them have definite hours for flight, the time depending particularly upon the flight period of the insects they prey upon. They retire for the day into dark situations such as hollow trees, caves, outhouses or under roofs. In these sleeping places great numbers often congregate, and several species may be represented. During bad weather, when their insect prey also remains under cover, they do not leave their daytime shelter. When asleep their body temperature falls considerably. In harmony with this nocturnal habit bats are usually dull coloured and are some tint of brown with the underside lighter than the upper.

All British species hibernate, and before the beginning of this period they develop a good deal of fat to carry them through it. This sleep is not always as continuous as was formerly supposed, and not only can the occasional bat be seen on the wing in winter, but it is now known that some bats move about within the roost, or go from one roost to another several miles away during the period of hibernation.

The larger bats usually eat their food as they fly, but the smaller bats rest for a few moments for this purpose. The web between the legs and tail (interfemoral pouch) is mostly used to catch their prey or hold it whilst it is being eaten. It also serves to receive the newly born young.

Recent investigations have shown that as well as being caught in the interfemoral membrane, used as a net, insects are sometimes caught directly in the mouth. In addition, bats have been seen to flex the third and fourth fingers, making a scoop with the wing-tip which directed insects into the mouth or the interfemoral membrane, or actually flicked them in.

The young vespertilionid bat is born blind and naked; the young horseshoe bat has sparse down on its back. It at once clings to its mother's fur by means of its claws, and hangs by its teeth to her nipple.

Nursing mothers appear to form colonies apart from the others. The growth of the young bat is rapid and it is soon fully covered with fur. At three weeks of age it takes its first flight, but it does not lead an independent life until it is about two months old. The longevity of bats was long in doubt, but recently up to twenty-one years have been recorded.

It seems certain that our bats are more numerous in the south becoming scarcer as we go west, and that there are few species represented in Scotland. Most of the species appear to be localized in distribution, the physical features of a district doubtless determining their local abundance or scarcity. They appear to be more numerous where there are woods, water and caves, as well as an abundance of insect life.

The Greater Horseshoe Bat

Family RHINOLOPHIDAE

*Rhinolophus
ferrum-equinum*

The distinguishing feature of horseshoe bats is the absence of the tragus from the ear and the presence of a leaf-like outgrowth of naked skin, known as the nose-leaf, on the muzzle around the nostrils. The broad forepart of this forms the horseshoe, a protruding central portion behind the nostrils is known as the sella, and behind it an erect tapering portion is the lancet. Horseshoe bats emit their pulses, in a narrow beam, through the nostrils instead of through the open mouth and the nose-leaf concentrates this beam and directs it in a searching movement. The pulses, therefore, travel much farther but with no greater effort than that of the

Greater horseshoe bats at their roost in a cave

bats lacking a nose-leaf. Greater horseshoe bats need this more effective echo-location since they fly low, down among bushes and herbage where they would be far more likely to collide with obstacles than in the upper air.

The greater horseshoe bat is heavily built and the female is usually larger than the male. The combined length of head and body is up to 70 mm and the length of the tail is 32 mm. The forearm is 51 mm long and the wing-span is up to 38 cm. The weight varies considerably throughout the year, the maximum being in December and the lowest in April. The large ears are about 16 mm broad, narrowing abruptly to the sharp recurved tip; when laid forward over the face they reach slightly beyond the tip of the muzzle. The mouth has a straight broad opening below the swollen muzzle with its stiff moustache. This bat's audible squeaks are sparrow-like chirps.

The lower portion of the broad wing membrane is attached to the ankle and the tail almost to the tip of the latter. The colour of the fur above is brownish and on the underside pale buff, often with a pinkish or yellowish tinge.

This bat emerges from its roost rather late in the evening and flies at intervals throughout the night. Its flight is heavy and butterfly-like, with frequent glides. Its food consists chiefly of beetles and moths as well as spiders. Small insects are devoured on the wing but the larger prey is usually taken to a resting-place to be eaten. It has been seen to settle on the ground, or on the stems of grass, and take ground-dwelling beetles such as the dor-beetle. It has also been seen on the ground lapping water.

It sleeps by day in caves, dark buildings, lofts and roofs. Hibernation, from October to the end of March, is usually in caves and tunnels. The bats hang singly or in groups, their presence overhead revealed by heaps of excrement on the ground below. Their natural resting attitude is hanging by the feet head downwards with the wings wrapped round the body. They cannot walk on a flat surface, and before alighting on a ceiling they turn a somersault in the air to get the proper position. Their senses are alert even when they are deep in winter sleep. They can appreciate a man's approach and will shrink from a finger pointed towards them at close range. They are highly temperature-sensitive and hibernation may begin earlier than October or end later than April, depending on weather conditions. Hibernation is not as continuous as has been previously supposed and there is a considerable amount of movement within the caves. Sometimes a bat will even move from one cave to another several kilometres away. When the air temperature outside rises to 10°C they will come out and feed on dung beetles.

There is one young at a birth, at the end of June or in July. Its eyes are closed, its underside is naked and the skin purple. The eyes open about the tenth day. The mother may at first take her baby out with her, clinging to her fur, when she goes foraging, or she may leave it hanging from the cave rafters together with other babies of the colony. How she manages to hang it up or retrieve it is not known.

This species is found chiefly in the southern half of England, especially in the south-west, and in south and west Wales. It does not occur in Scotland or Ireland.

The Lesser Horseshoe Bat

Family RHINOLOPHIDAE   *Rhinolophus hipposideros*

The lesser horseshoe bat is much smaller and more delicately built than the greater horseshoe bat, and its nose-leaf has a narrower outline. The head and body length is 39 mm and that of the forearm is about the same. The wing-span is less than 25·4 cm. The maximum weight is in December and the lowest in April. The colour is much the same as in the larger species, but somewhat greyer brown, without the yellow or pink below, and the fur is longer and more silky. Its habits are similar also, but it does not hunt such large beetles, nor does it fly so low. It has a more fluttering flight with intervals of gliding.

Lesser horseshoe bat at roost

Breeding habits are similar to those of the greater horseshoe. The single young is born in June or July, with a thin coat of downy hair on the upper side only.

The species appears to be more abundant where there are caves which provide the equable temperature needed in hibernation. This lasts from October to the beginning of April but is not continuous, the bats often shifting their quarters within the cave, and possibly feeding then on gnats over-wintering in the cave. The lesser horseshoe bat is most susceptible to wind, and will frequently remain inactive in its summer shelter because there is wind outside.

It is a common species in the south of England, from Kent to Cornwall, although scarce in Sussex and Hampshire. It is still common, but more sparingly, in Wales, very rare in East Anglia and rare in the Midlands, its northward range terminating at Ripon, in Yorkshire. In Ireland it occurs in the west only.

The Whiskered Bat

Family VESPERTILIONIDAE *Myotis mystacinus*

The small and usually solitary whiskered bat is frequently confused with the pipistrelle which, however, is smaller and has a broader muzzle. The head and body measure up to 50 mm and the tail is the same length. The forearm is 38 mm long. The wings are narrow and have a span of 24 cm. The weight of a fully grown individual varies from 4·5–6 g.

The soft, long fur of the upper parts is dark or smoky brown which may be nearly black, and the under surface is lighter, the hairs being tipped with white. In young individuals the underside also is dark brown. The fur extends but slightly on to the wing membrane, and there is little of it on the long, slender ear, whose outer margin is deeply notched. The straight, tapering tragus is half the length of the shell of the ear. The hinder margin of the brownish black wing membrane is continued to the base of the toes, and the spur (calcar) reaches halfway from the

35

ankle to the long tail. Owing to the length of the fur on the face, the small eyes are almost hidden and the face appears to be very short. There is a bristly moustache on the upper lip which has suggested its common and scientific names.

This bat is usually solitary but has been seen in colonies of up to a hundred or more in both summer and winter. It makes its appearance early in the evening, flying low along hedgerows, plantations and cliffs, its method of hunting being not to chase flying insects in the air but to pick off those which have settled on leaves and twigs. It may also be seen at times flying in the daytime. It prefers the neighbourhood of woods and water, where it finds many flies, beetles and moths in flight. Its voice is a low, buzzing squeak but it is quite silent on the wing.

The flight of the whiskered bat is slow, steady and silent. They appear not to wander far but keep to a single pool or short stretches of a stream, where they flit about among the trees, such as alders, usually at a height of about 7 m. Often they fly within a few centimetres of the ground or skim the surface of a pool for a metre or two.

Whiskered bats roost in hollow trees, under loose bark, in a hole in the wall, a roof, or behind window shutters. Hibernation, which lasts from November to March, is in a cave, rock fissure or cellar, from which individuals may emerge for a brief flight whenever the weather is fine.

On the wing it is not easily distinguished from the pipistrelle which is so similar in size; but the noisiness of the pipistrelle compared with the silence of the whiskered bat is the best guide.

The solitary young one is born in June or July.

The whiskered bat is widely distributed through-

Whiskered bat in flight

out England, with the exception of East Anglia, where it is rare. In Yorkshire it has been found at an elevation of 425 m. It appears to be rare in south Wales, but common in north Wales and also in Ireland. It is very rare in Scotland.

There are four other representatives of the genus *Myotis* in the British Isles, the whiskered bat being the smallest member. They are all of slender, delicate form, which is seen most clearly in the shape of the skull, the muzzle, the ear and its tragus.

Natterer's Bat

Family VESPERTILIONIDAE   *Myotis nattereri*

The Natterer's or red-grey bat is somewhat larger over the spread wings than the whiskered bat, but the head and body measure about the same, up to 50 mm. The forearm is 38 mm long. The tail is relatively short, being only 38 mm. The wing-span is up to 28·5 cm.

The long, soft and dense fur is of a greyish-brown colour above and whitish on the underside, with a distinct line of demarcation from the base of the ear to the shoulder. The wing membranes are dusky. This bat has a small head, with a narrow muzzle which is naked at the tip and slightly overhangs the lower jaw. The face is so densely covered with fur that the small eyes are hidden. There are also moustachial bristles above the lips on each side arising from a prominent gland. The large oval ear is notched on the outer margin above the middle, and the long slender tragus is more than half the length of the ear, ending in a long, very slender point. It has a deep notch near the base on its hind

Natterer's bat in flight

margin. The wing membrane extends to the base of the outer toe, and the interfemoral membrane is distinctly fringed with stiff hairs along its lower edge. In flight the tail is directed downwards at an angle of sixty degrees or more.

The Natterer's bat shares the whiskered bat's partiality for wooded districts. It is both sociable and gregarious, and its daytime retreat in holes in walls, hollow trees and caverns, is shared with bats of its own and other species. It emerges early in the evening and hunts intermittently through the night. It flies low, with a slow, steady flight, and often picks flies and small moths off leaves and twigs.

The solitary young one is born towards the end of June or early in July. Hibernation ends in March, and it begins, in caves, during December. Surprisingly, this bat is often solitary in hibernation.

Natterer's bat is generally distributed over England, being plentiful in many counties. It also occurs in Wales and is widely distributed in Ireland, but is only occasionally recorded in Scotland.

Bechstein's Bat

Family VESPERTILIONIDAE   *Myotis bechsteini*

Bechstein's bat has a general resemblance to Natterer's bat, but is slightly larger, with ears almost twice the breadth and the feet larger. The ears are relatively larger than those of any European bat, except the long-eared bat. The wings are narrow and pointed towards the tips.

The body is covered with soft, woolly fur, which is a greyish-brown on the upper parts and buff-grey below. The membranes are dark brown; that of the

Bechstein's bat in flight

wing reaches to the base of the toes, and that of the interfemoral leaves the last joint of the tail free.

The combined length of head and body is about 50 mm; the tail is 38 mm. The forearm is nearly 44 mm long. The ears are 20–26 mm in length and 13 mm wide; the tragus is half the length of the ear. The span of the wings is 25 cm. The few records of weight are for approximately 7–13 g. The single young is born about midsummer.

Bechstein's is the rarest of British bats and up to 1946 it had been recorded only from the south of England, the localities being the New Forest, Isle of Wight, Sussex, Berkshire and Oxfordshire. It has since been recorded from Devon, Dorset, Somerset, Gloucestershire, Wiltshire and Shropshire. Our knowledge of its habits is derived chiefly from the

Continent, where it flies about woods, orchards and the neighbourhood of dwellings, coming out from its retreat late in the evening and flying slowly and low over lanes and woodland roads, but only in calm weather.

It lives in small colonies in summer, roosting in hollow trees or in buildings (e.g. in roof spaces). Its voice is a low buzz, or a high-pitched squeal, when excited. It feeds mainly on moths taken on the wing or picked off leaves.

Hibernation is in caves but other retreats are almost certainly used, although information on this is lacking.

The Mouse-eared Bat

Family VESPERTILIONIDAE   *Myotis myotis*

Although this bat has been found in England, it is mainly only a rare winter immigrant from the Continent, occasionally becoming temporarily resident, with two colonizations in Dorset and Sussex.

It is larger than any of our native species, measuring 63–91 mm head and body, with a wing-span of 35–45 cm. The forearm is 51–68 mm long. The ears are 19 mm broad and 25 mm long, and when laid forward extend beyond the muzzle. The mouse-eared bat is medium-brown above and greyish-white beneath, with a clear line of demarcation from the base of the ear to the shoulder. Its roosts are in caves and buildings.

Investigations in 1959 found that the droppings of these bats contained considerable remains of non-flying insects and spiders. The bats were observed hopping over the ground, apparently locating dung beetles by smell. (Bat illustrated on page 42.)

Mouse-eared bat

Daubenton's Bat

Family VESPERTILIONIDAE   *Myotis daubentoni*

Daubenton's or the water bat was formerly considered one of our rarest bats, but is known now to
be both widely distributed and plentiful. It had
probably been mistaken for the common bat or
pipistrelle to which it is similar in size, though its
habits are different. It keeps close to the water,

especially to some alder-sheltered pool in the river where there are plenty of caddis-flies and other insects. There, from soon after sunset, it flies in circles, with a slow, quivering flight, frequently dipping its muzzle in the water to pick up surface insects. In such places the evening fly-fisher sometimes finds this bat caught on his hook. It appears to be on the wing all night, but individuals are not continuously active, their night being spent in bursts of activity followed by periods of rest. It was probably to this bat that Gilbert White referred in his eleventh letter to Pennant, when he said: 'As I was going, some years ago, pretty late, in a boat from Richmond to Sunbury, on a warm summer's evening, I think I saw myriads of bats between the two places.' This was long before it had been distinguished as a distinct species, and when it would probably have been regarded as the common bat.

Albino Daubenton's bat. Albinism in bats is rare

It has short, dense fur, of a grizzled warm brown colour on the upper parts, and lighter brown or buffy grey, sometimes so pale as to show a distinct line of separation, along the sides from the angle of the lips to the thigh. The face is dusky, and the ears and wing membrane are of a reddish dusky tint. The interfemoral membrane is whitish below, and there are whitish hairs on the toes. The membrane arises from the middle of the foot.

Daubenton's bat is a little larger than the whiskered bat and the common bat. The head and body measure about 50 mm, the tail 32 mm, the ear 12 mm and the forearm 36 mm; the wing-span is about 25 cm. The few records of weight are for about 7–11 g. The lower hindleg and foot are conspicuously large. The ear has a rounded tip, and a shallow concavity on the upper part of the hind margin; the lance-shaped tragus is about half the length of the ear. The spur or calcar of the foot extends three-quarters of the distance between the foot and the tail. The last two joints of the latter usually extend beyond the membrane.

In summer this bat roosts in the daytime in crevices in trees, walls, caves or roofs, often in numbers. It emerges late in the evening and up to two hundred have been seen over one lake. It is usually silent on the wing, but gives an angry buzz when alarmed. In hibernation—which extends from the end of September to about the middle of April— it is no longer sociable, but hangs alone in some dark cave or in a building, or in groups of up to half a dozen.

There is a single young one, born in June or July.

The range of this species extends from Ireland to Asia, and from the Mediterranean to central Norway.

The Pipistrelle or Common Bat

Family VESPERTILIONIDAE   *Pipistrellus pipistrellus*

The pipistrelle or common bat is in a general sense familiar to everybody, for it may be seen in the evenings flying everywhere, even in the streets of crowded cities. Its British distribution extends from the south of England to Scotland and the Hebrides, and westwards to Ireland. Its wider range includes Europe and parts of Asia. It is the smallest of the British bats.

Pipistrelles in their roost

In spite of its small size—the head and body measuring little more than 38 mm with just over 50 mm as the maximum—the pipistrelle is of robust build, and it has a wing-span of 20–23 cm. Its fore-arm measures 35 mm and it weighs up to 7·5 g. The female is slightly larger than the male. The pipistrelle has a flat, broad head with a blunt muzzle and wide mouth. The short, broad ears, somewhat triangular with blunt tips and with outer edges slightly notched, end just behind the angle of the mouth. The tail is little over 25 mm in length, and the legs also are short. The last joint of the tail is free from the membrane and prehensile, and the bat is said to make use of it as a support in crawling up or down a vertical surface. The spur reaches more than halfway to the tail, and an important identification feature is the lobe of membrane behind the spur, known as the post-calcarial lobe. The narrow wing is attached to the middle of the sole of the foot.

The somewhat silky fur is a reddish brown on the upper parts and slightly paler beneath. The wing membrane and the ears are blackish.

This is a very active bat, flying with a rapid, jerky flight, at heights between 1·8 to 12·2 m from the ground, on a regular beat over farmyards and gardens and about houses, frequently uttering its shrill little squeak as it snaps up the flies and small beetles, pouching and eating them without alighting.

It was formerly supposed that it continued its flight all through the night, but the likelihood is that its activity is intermittent, with periods of rest away from the roost. It has a longer period of activity over the year than any other species, for it leaves its place of hibernation in March and does not retire until the end of October or November. Even then, a moderately high midday temperature is sufficient to awaken it and bring it out for an hour's hunt.

It has a wide choice of sleeping places and is frequently found under roofs, behind rain-water pipes and gutters, or in any crevices between woodwork and brickwork in buildings, as well as in hollow trees and crevices in rocks.

Mating takes place prior to hibernation, and fertilization is delayed until the following spring. One young one is born, usually in late June to mid-July, sometimes in August.

The Serotine Bat

Family VESPERTILIONIDAE   *Eptesicus serotinus*

The serotine and the noctule are our two largest bats, and in the early records they were very much confused. In both, the wing-span may reach 38 cm. Though similar in size, they may be known apart by the shape of the ear; in the serotine it is oval-triangular with the tips rounded. The fur is also of a darker brown, and there are other points of difference, such as the possession of two additional teeth by the noctule, and the interior pre-molar being absent from the upper jaw of the serotine. In flight the much broader wings of the serotine are the best features for identification.

The serotine has a somewhat swollen face with little hair on the front portion, apart from a moustache on the upper lip; but owing to the dark skin of the face the lack of fur is not very noticeable. The dark brown fur of the upper parts is soft and dense; behind the shoulders the hairs have buffy tips. On the underside the fur is somewhat lighter. There is little extension of fur on the wing, except a line of down on the undersurface of the forearm. The wing-membrane is attached to the base of the toes. The head and body measure about 76 mm and the tail slightly exceeds 50 mm, the last joint being quite free of the membrane. The forearm measures 50 mm. The wing-span is 33–38 cm. The weight is up to 33 g, the female being slightly larger. There are prominent glandular swellings on the muzzle. The ear is about 19 mm long; the short tragus—less than half the length of ear—has a straight front border and a curved hind border, with rounded tip.

This bat makes its appearance about sunset, but may emerge at any time during the following hour, for a flight of about half an hour. Then it takes a rest and after that hunts intermittently through the night. It frequents glades in woods, and preys upon beetles and moths. In May and June large numbers of cockchafers fall victims to it, and in July and August, in Kent and Sussex, it plays havoc with the local brown-tail moth. It eats on the wing, and also at rest. In the early part of its season it flies at a low height, but later it prefers an altitude between 9 to 12 m from which, however, it frequently descends to the ground. The change is, no doubt, connected with the seasonal succession of insects with different habits. This bat is gregarious and when it retires to holes or roofs for its daytime rest it is usually in companies of up to twenty, but it may roost solitarily. Before leaving for a night's foraging serotines are known to cluster. Usually silent, it sometimes utters in flight a strident squeak described as *tick-tick*.

Hibernation is from mid-October until April or May, sometimes mid-March, in hollow trees, in buildings or under loose bark on old or dead trees. Sleep is continuous but the bat has been seen to take wing readily if disturbed.

Not a great deal is known about the breeding habits of the serotine. It is thought that a single young is born in June, perhaps sometimes in May, and that this takes its first flight at the age of three weeks.

Except for a few records of its occurrence in Essex, Cambridgeshire, Suffolk, Middlesex, Hertfordshire, Cornwall and Glamorgan, it is restricted to that part of England bounded by the River Thames and the English Channel, including the Isle of Wight but not Devon. Even in these places it is

Serotine at roost. (Note band on right forearm)

only abundant locally. Kent is its main stronghold and there it is the commonest bat. Outside the British Isles, it extends through central and south Europe, from Denmark to the Mediterannean and eastward into temperate Asia. It also occurs in Tunisia and Algeria.

The Noctule or Great Bat

Family VESPERTILIONIDAE *Nyctalus noctula*

Though similar to the serotine in size and to the pipistrelle in form, the noctule or great bat was recognized as a distinct species by Gilbert White in the eighteenth century, who first called attention to it under the name of *altivolans*, suggested by its high flight. Schreber, however, had some years previously named it *noctula*, basing his description upon a French specimen.

The general form of the noctule is robust and heavy, the forearm massive, the wing long and slender, its narrowness being due to the shortness of the fifth finger. The lower leg is short and thick, and the foot broad and powerful. The muzzle is broad and has a glandular swelling between eye and nostril. The nostrils project forward and outward, and there is a distinct concavity between the two crescent-shaped orifices. The ear is short—when flattened it is broader than long—with the front border rounded to the tip; its inner surface is covered with short hairs. The ears are spaced widely apart. There is a very short, downy, bow-shaped tragus, broader above than below. The long, soft, golden-brown fur is thick, and extends over the face and a short distance over the wing; it is paler and duller on the lower parts. On the underside there is a narrow band of fur below the arm bones. The last joint of the tail is free. The membrane and ears are blackish.

The head and body together measure up to 82 mm in length. The forearm is 50 mm long. The wing-span is 35–38 cm. The weight is unusually

Noctule bats at roost

variable from 16–39 g, and the female is larger than the male.

The noctule, as one would expect from the shape of the wings, has a quick, dashing flight recalling that of the swifts, with which, indeed, it may sometimes be seen high in the air hawking for the same prey. It often glides down obliquely on expanded wings. It flies at twilight and again at dawn, as well as in the daytime occasionally. It has a shrill, clear, cricket-like voice when hunting and a strident screech when excited.

C. B. Moffat wrote that they 'cram themselves to bursting point either once or twice in the twenty-four hours, during a seventy minutes' career of mad excitement among the twilight-flying beetles and gnats'. They also take moths and other insects, but in captivity they have resolutely refused to eat such warningly coloured species as the cinnabar and magpie moths. It has been shown that at one meal they will consume food equal to a quarter of their own weight. When one considers the lightness of insects, the impact of these purely insectivorous animals on the insect population must be considerable.

Their roosts are in hollow trees and under the eaves of buildings, where anything up to one or two hundred individuals may associate together especially in hibernation. Their presence is often indicated by thick layers of excrement beneath their roosting places. Some colonies change their roosts at frequent but irregular intervals, especially in June and July, with the result that noctules may sometimes be seen making long flights.

Individual noctules may be seen in flight all through the year, with the exception of January and the latter part of December, but hibernation generally lasts from October to the middle or end of March.

The sexes are said to separate into distinct colonies in the early summer, the females retiring into hollow trees to bear and rear their young. Mating takes place from August to October but there is a pause in the development of the embryo during hibernation, and the single young born naked and blind is not delivered until the end of June. Within a month it is independent of the mother. When they first get their fur they are much darker than the adult. Twins are not uncommon on the continent, and triplets have twice been recorded.

Although the noctule is generally distributed as far north as Yorkshire, Durham and the Lake District, it is common only in the southern half of England, from Norfolk to Cornwall, but is rare in the Isle of Wight. It is not recorded from Ireland. Formerly, it was not considered a native of Scotland, but in recent years several examples have been captured there. It is found throughout the greater part of Europe and parts of Asia.

Leisler's Bat

Family VESPERTILIONIDAE   *Nyctalus leisleri*

Leisler's or the hairy-winged bat is smaller than the noctule and darker. The length of the head and body is 63 mm and of the tail 38 mm. The forearm is about 44 mm. The wing-span is 25–30 cm. The weight is 14–20 g. The fur on the upper parts is a darker brown than that of the noctule, but it is lighter on the underparts. The skull is only half the size of that of the noctule, and the entire build is lighter and

Leisler's bat in flight

less massive. It flies more at the level of the pipistrelle, 3–15 m, but its movements are not so swift
and are more zigzag.

It is one of the rarest of our bats, and is a woodland
species, making its roost preferably high up in a
decayed oak, but also in the roofs and crevices of
buildings. It is given to changing its roosts frequently. Often gregarious, in colonies of up to a
hundred, it is at times solitary, especially during
hibernation, which lasts from October to mid-April,
but a little mild weather in winter will wake it up
and bring it out for a flight. The evening flight lasts
for about an hour, starting just after sunset, and
there is a second flight of a similar period starting
just before sunrise. Its food consists of flies, beetles

and moths, which it consumes so rapidly on the wing that it returns gorged to its roost.

The single young is born in June.

The distribution of Leisler's bat does not agree at all with that of the noctule. It has been recorded for Devon, Somerset, Gloucestershire, Hampshire, Surrey, Kent, Essex, Hertfordshire, Cambridgeshire, Norfolk, Northamptonshire, Warwickshire, Worcestershire, Cheshire and Yorkshire. It does not appear to occur in Scotland, but was formerly reported as abundant in several parts of Ireland.

The Long-eared Bat

Family VESPERTILIONIDAE *Plecotus auritus*

The long-eared is probably the best-known of our bats, with its huge ears, as long as the forearm and longer than the body. In addition it is one of the commonest and most widely distributed bats, likely to be met with anywhere in the British Islands, although somewhat rarer in the Highlands of Scotland than elsewhere. It is found nearly all over Europe.

The large and mobile ears give this bat an appearance of size not justified by its small and delicate build. The head and body combined measure up to 50 mm and the tail is only a fraction less. The forearm measures 38 mm. The weight ranges from 5–12 g. The long ears have their bases joined across the top of the head and their outer margins end just behind the angle of the mouth. Each is a long oval with rounded tip. Except for fringes on the folds they are hairless. They are semi-transparent and marked with conspicuous transverse folds. The tapering tragus is nearly half as long as the ear, and might be mistaken for it when the bat hangs asleep, for then the ears are carefully folded and tucked away in the wing whilst the tragus sticks out beyond the inanimate-looking bundle. Sometimes, when the bat is awake, one ear is held at a different angle from the other, but in flight both ears are directed forward. Sometimes when the bat is partly awake, the ears are curled sideways and then appear similar to rams' horns.

The soft, silky, brown fur is long and thick, especially on the shoulders, but does not extend on to the surface of the wings. On the underparts it pales to light brown or dirty white. The wings are both long and broad, and their span is about 25 cm. The long tail when folded forwards can touch the top of the head; its tip is slightly free from the inter-femoral membrane, and when the bat hangs head downwards for sleep it serves as an extra hook for suspension.

The long-eared bat is found chiefly among trees, though it sometimes comes into open windows at night. It flies among the branches of trees, where it picks insects off the leaves. Its flight is then a glide punctuated with hovering. In passing from one tree to another it flies swiftly and strongly close to the ground and often, when it has caught an insect, it will land on the ground to eat it. In early spring, when the sallows are in bloom and attracting swarms of insects, the long-eared bat is there also. It appears in the evening, usually about half an hour after sunset, and intermittent flights are made throughout the night, until about an hour before sunrise. Occasionally it may be seen in the daytime. It appears to be at least partially migratory, for it has been observed that in summer a swarm will appear in a district where they are not noticeable as a rule, and after staying a few weeks disappear. A report some years ago tells of a group of long-eared bats, coming from the direction of Scandinavia, that settled on a ship in the North Sea and took off at dusk, heading for the English coast.

Long-eared bat at roost

The single young one is born in June or July.

The breeding females often associate in large numbers, away from the males, while they are nursing.

Hibernation lasts from the middle of November until early April but should the thermometer register 7·7°C or more at any time during the winter, the long-eared bat awakes and makes a foraging flight—calling attention to its presence by an acute, shrill cry. On the other hand, it may move its quarters within the cave without necessarily coming into the open.

These bats are often found hibernating in clusters in caves or even under house-roofs; but solitary individuals are also found in hollow trees and similar situations.

The Grey Long-eared Bat

Family VESPERTILIONIDAE   *Plecotus austriacus*

The presence of this European bat in England was first recognized in 1964 from a specimen deposited in the British Museum collection in 1875. It had been discovered at Netley, Hampshire, and another was caught at Christchurch in 1909. Since 1964 there have been twenty-four further captures, all in Dorset. This species and the common long-eared are so alike that there is still some doubt whether the two are specifically different. The grey is said to be more aggressive, biting when handled, in contrast to the docile temperament of the common species. The face of the grey is dark to very dark brown, almost black, that of the common being flesh-coloured to light brown.

Barbastelle at roost

The Barbastelle

Family VESPERTILIONIDAE *Barbastella barbastellus*

The barbastelle is a medium-sized bat of slender form with relatively long legs and small feet. The ears are large, being as broad as they are long, and united by their bases just behind the muzzle. The lance-shaped tragus is half the length of the ear, and has two notches towards the base of the hind margin.

The long, soft fur is a very dark brown, but many

of the hairs on the upper surface have pale tips which give a frosted appearance. This continues on both surfaces of the wings and the interfemoral membrane. The wing, ear, nose and foot are dusky, appearing lighter than the furred regions, and the undersurface is slightly lighter than the upper.

The head and body measure about 50 mm and the tail 44 mm. The forearm measures 38 mm. The wing-span is about 26 cm. The weight is from 6–8 g. This and the long-eared bat are the only British species in which the ears are connected, and the form of the ear in each is so distinct that there is no danger of confusing them. It is both solitary and silent in flight, which begins early in the evening, often in daylight, is continuous until midnight and then intermittent until just before dawn. While in the air it holds its feet far apart and the tail decurved. In fine weather it flies high. During its daytime rest it has been found in various retreats, often in company: under thatch of a shed, between the rafters and tiles of outhouses, in the crevices of walls and trees. Its voice is a metallic squeak or a deep buzz.

Hibernation begins in September and lasts until early April. Nothing is known of its breeding.

The barbastelle is found chiefly in the South of England, and elsewhere is confined to England and Wales.

The Fox

Family CANIDAE   *Vulpes vulpes*

It is usually assumed that, except in the wildest and most remote corners of our island, the fox would long ago have been extinct but for its careful preservation by the various 'hunts'. As far back as the reign of Elizabeth I, an Act of Parliament was passed for the protection of grain, which incidentally pro-

Vixen. (Note elliptical pupils to eyes)

vided for a bounty of twelve pence for the head of every fox or grey (badger). Today, outside the hunt areas, the killing of a fox is considered a meritorious act, particularly in the northern mountain districts. Yet, in spite of all, the fox has survived, due mainly to its ability to look after itself.

The head and body of the fox measures usually a little over 61 cm in length and the bushy white-tipped tail or brush adds up to 40 cm to its length, but examples have been recorded greatly exceeding these measurements, especially in Scotland. It stands only about 35 cm at the shoulder. An average dog fox weighs 6·8 kg, a vixen 5·4 kg.

The beautiful fur is sandy, russet or red-brown above and white on the underparts. The back of the ears is black and usually also the front of the limbs. These are the typical colours but there is a great deal of variation in colour between one individual and another.

The sharp-pointed long muzzle, the erect ears and the quick movements of the eye with its elliptical pupil, combine to give the fox an alert, cunning appearance, which so impressed the ancient writers that they invented many stories of its astuteness. Dog-fox and vixen are similar in appearance, the vixen being slightly smaller and also distinguished by a narrower face since she lacks the cheek ruffs of the male.

Foxes are largely nocturnal and, except at the breeding season, lead solitary lives. Most of the day is spent in an 'earth' which is often acquired from a badger or rabbit. In the former instance the fox probably takes up quarters in the entrance to a badger's set and makes it uninhabitable to the more cleanly beast by permeating it with the secretion

Year-old dog fox

from glands under the tail. In the case of the rabbit burrow, the fox gets undisputed possession by eating out those who constructed it. Foxes in captivity show a strong tendency to dig, and when allowed semi-freedom will construct earths readily by their own efforts. They always make at least two openings to the earth, although it is usually said that a wild fox stops all exits to its earth except one.

Now that rabbits are scarcer, the fox's chief items of food are rats, mice and also bank voles. Hedgehogs, squirrels, voles, frogs, even snails and beetles, as well as a great deal of vegetable matter are also eaten. Birds will be taken, and pheasant, partridge, poultry and even lambs clearly do fall victim. These

63

habits, however, tend to be local. A vixen that has taken to killing poultry will teach her cubs to do the same, and doubtless something of the sort happens with lambs, but there are many instances of foxes repeatedly visiting poultry farms and never molesting the birds.

During winter, at night the characteristic barking of the fox can be heard, and the 'scream of the vixen' is an eerie sound in the dark. Apart from these, foxes use a great variety of calls. It has long been thought that only the vixen screams, but the dog-fox also does. And the scream may be heard at any time of the year.

Mating takes place from late December to February. Once they have mated, the dog and vixen keep close together and there is a great deal of playing between them. About April the vixen produces her single litter of, usually, four cubs. They are blind until ten days old, and remain in the earth until nearly a month old, the vixen staying close with them, while the dog supplies much of the food. When nearly a month old they are taken out one night for exercise and can sometimes be seen playing as a group with the parents outside the earth, and this continues for several weeks. Later, the vixen takes them out and teaches them to hunt. In due course, the cubs tend to wander and this, combined with the vixen's increasing irritability, ensures that ultimately they do not return. The cubs reach adult size six months after birth.

Foxes are said to resort to a particular stratagem to attain their end which has been called 'charming'. A story is usually told of a fox rolling about to attract a group of rabbits feeding nearby. Then it begins chasing its tail while the silly rabbits gaze spellbound at the performance. All the time the fox contrives to get nearer, until a sudden straightening of the body enables it to grab the nearest rabbit in its jaws. It is more likely, however, that charming is not a deliberate strategy. Foxes are naturally playful and a fox finding that birds and rabbits are attracted to it, might use it again with more deliberation.

The red fox ranges over Europe and Asia as far south as central India. It is found throughout the British Isles at all levels, except for Orkney and Shetland and all Scottish islands other than Skye. The foxes of the northern hill country are said to be a finer race than those of the southern woodlands.

The Badger

Family MUSTELIDAE   *Meles meles*

The badger is, with the hedgehog, our most completely nocturnal animal. It is sometimes seen abroad during the day, but on the whole it comes out regularly after sunset and goes home again at dawn. Its habit of living deep in the earth is in its favour, and above all it keeps very much out of the way. There must be many people who have lived near a family of badgers without suspecting their presence. Badgers are even living in the parks of outer London, unbeknown to the majority of visitors.

The badger measures 75–93 cm long and stands about 30 cm high at the shoulder. At a short distance its rough coat appears a uniform grey, but on closer inspection it is seen to be somewhat reddish on the back and black underneath. There is something almost pig-like about the stout, squat body, yet its gait is more reminiscent of that of a bear. The legs are short, there are five toes on each foot and the front paws, more especially, are armed with powerful claws. Its weight may be up to 18 kg or even more, and for its size it is immensely strong.

The most striking feature is the head, with its long tapering muzzle marked with broad bands of white, and with a black band running from the ear to the snout, on each side of the head. The eyes and ears are both small. A badger has an acute sense of smell and good hearing but its sight is poor. The badger's peculiar jaw gives it a tenacious grip. The lower jaw is permanently hinged to the skull and cannot be dislocated without breaking the bone of the skull.

The badger's diet is fairly wide. It will take acorns, beech mast and other wild fruits, eat grass and clover, and dig for roots. It will also eat earthworms, slugs and beetles, and the larvae of beetles and moths. It will dig out the nests of bumblebees and wasps for the grubs and take larger prey such as young rabbits, lizards, mice, voles, young birds and even still-born lambs. It has also been known to maul carcasses of deer.

The badger's underground home, known as a set, may be 3 m or more below the surface, with a main entrance sloping down to the passages and upper and lower galleries, with probably a back door at some distance from the main entrance. The main opening is marked by a mound of earth, turned out during the excavation, and the size of this gives some indication of the depth and extent of the set. The cubs, of which there are normally two or three but may be one or five, are usually born in February in a special breeding chamber in the set, furnished with moss and grass. The litters are born occasionally as early as mid-January or as late as May. Under normal conditions the cubs remain below ground for six to eight weeks after birth.

The newly-born cub is just under 12 cm long, blind and a dirty white in colour, with no hair on the undersides. The eyes open at about ten days. At first the head stripes are faint, but about the time the eyes open the hair is becoming darker, and a light grey, and the dark lines on the head become more emphasized. For a time, after first coming above ground, the cubs do not wander far from the entrance to the set. The mother comes out first and, if the coast is clear, will turn back into the entrance, possibly calling the cubs out. At the slightest disturbance they will bolt back into the entrance.

At about eleven weeks the cubs become more

Badger's set

Badger and cub leaving set

active and begin to play more, but they are still very wary. They are weaned a week or so after this, but they remain with the sow until autumn, and sometimes throughout the winter.

Badgers in this country do not hibernate although they may be less active in the winter. They are said to hibernate partially in the colder parts of Europe.

It is often said that the white markings on the badger's face are protective because they harmonize with the light and shadow of a moonlit night. Badgers, however, avoid moonlit nights by keeping underground, or using dense cover. More likely these are recognition marks by which the animals can see each other, in the darkness of the set or above ground.

Badgers are proverbially clean animals. They use latrines dug in the ground at a distance from the set or they may have special chambers in the set for these. In January and February the set is spring-cleaned and old bedding renewed.

A small badger cub makes a high-pitched whickering, and a loud squeal when alarmed. Cubs playing make puppy-like noises. Adults growl or bark as a warning and purr with pleasure, and both boar and sow will scream, a long-drawn eerie sound, often for no obvious reason.

Badgers are present in every county in England, Wales and Ireland, and in most counties of Scotland, although not very common in the Highlands.

The Otter

Family MUSTELIDAE   *Lutra lutra*

Otters are seen more often by luck than by persistent searching and most people have to confess to never having seen one in the wild. One may meet one accidentally, perhaps in the headlights of a car, or by long searching by night along the banks of remote streams or tarns, where there are alder-holts, or in the neighbourhood of the East Anglian Broads. An otter may sometimes be found by day in summer, lying up in the caves on some remote part of our coast where the cliffs are rocky and the shore strewn with boulders. The occasional otter was formerly seen in the Thames, in the neighbourhood of the heavily built-up areas of London.

The long, lithe body of the otter ending in the long tapering tail is streamlined for swimming. The head

69

is broad and flattened from above, the face short, the black eyes small but bright and the short, rounded ears hairy. The ears are closed when under water. The legs are short and powerful, and all the feet are completely webbed. There are five toes on each, those on the forefeet having short pointed claws. The tail is somewhat flattened from the sides, and forms a most efficient rudder. Below its thick base there is a pair of glands which secrete a most objectionable fluid. The fur is of two kinds: a fine, soft waterproof underfur of whitish-grey with brown tips, among which are interspersed longer, thicker, and glossy hairs, the so-called guard-hairs. On the upper parts and the outer sides of the limbs, these longer hairs, which have a grey base, have rich brown ends; but on the cheeks, throat, and underparts they are light brown to silvery grey.

The total length is about 1·2 m, exceptionally up to 1·8 m, of which one-third is tail. The weight of a full-grown male is 9–12 kg. There are records of 23 kg and one of almost 27 kg.

Its holt or lair will probably be a hole in the bank with the entrance under water and overhung by alders and rank herbage, but it may be well away from water. The holt is used only for the time that cubs are present; at other times an otter has no permanent home. There may be an alternative way in at the back of the bank above water. The otter rests in the daytime in the holt or in reed beds, coiled up like a dog with its tail around its face. The spraints, or droppings, are a good clue to the otter's presence.

An otter starts its hunting about sunset when its flute-like whistle can be heard. It hunts favourite pools in the stream for fish, which are always

Otter swimming

brought to the bank to be eaten. The backbone is first bitten through behind the gills; and where fish are large and plentiful, the otter often contents itself with a mouthful from the shoulder. At other times it may eat methodically from this point to the tail, which is always left. Apart from the fact that it has to make frequent visits to the surface in order to breathe, it is as much at home in the water as a fish, swimming in circles where the water is deep, and its movements in that element are as graceful as those of the fishes it pursues. An important item in its diet is eels. Occasionally it may take wild duck or moorhen; and when it hunts on land, rabbits, rats, mice and voles. Frogs, newts and freshwater shrimps are also eaten, and on land slugs, earthworms and beetles. A favourite food is crayfish. When it goes downstream it floats with the current, its forelegs pressed against its sides and only the upper parts of the head with eyes, ears and nostrils exposed.

In summer when the water is low in the streams, it travels across country from pool to pool by night, to an estuary or the open coast. Although so obviously adapted for an aquatic life, the otter can travel with speed on land, and it has been estimated that in one night it will cover about 24 km. On arrival at the coast it will use a cave as a shelter, from which it will work the shallow waters for flatfish, bass, crabs and mussels. In autumn it will return to its usual inland haunts, perhaps taking migrating eels on the way. Otters do not hibernate.

Not much is known of their breeding habits. There seems to be no fixed breeding season, the young being born at all times of the year. A nursery nest or 'hover' is constructed of rushes and grass, and lined with the soft, purple flower panicles of the great reed. In Norfolk the nursery is frequently found on the surface of the water, in the great reed-beds. There are two or three cubs in a litter born blind but already covered with a fine downy fur. Both parents hunt to provide them with food, and they remain in the hover for several weeks before being taken out one night to be taught their way about in the water. It is believed that the partnership of the parents is only temporary, and as soon as the young ones are capable of taking care of themselves, the dog otter goes to live by himself.

Otters, like other carnivores, are given to playing. They will often give a low pitched chortle of pleasure. Other vocalisations are the whickering of the cubs, and, in the adult, the long drawn out moan of apprehension, and a hiss or high-pitched chatter of annoyance.

Widespread in Britain, but probably more rare than formerly, the otter ranges across Europe and North Africa.

The Pine Marten

Family MUSTELIDAE   *Martes martes*

The pine marten or marten cat was formerly quite a common woodland beast, but owing to persecution and the high prices paid for a skin, it is now found only in the wilder parts of the Lake District, the North of England, Wales, Scotland and Ireland, and in some of these places appears to be increasing in numbers.

The pine marten resembles the better-known stoat but is larger with longer legs, a broader, more triangular head with sharp-pointed muzzle, and a longer more bushy tail. Its entire length is between 63–76 cm, of which 25–28 cm is tail; the females are slightly smaller than the males. The weight of an adult ranges from 0·9–1·5 kg. Its colour is a rich dark brown, except on the throat and breast where the colour varies from orange through yellow to creamy-white. The middle of the back and the exposed sides of the legs and feet are darker than the rest of the body, and the underparts are greyish. The superficial colour is provided by the long upper, glossy fur, but beneath this is a finer, softer fur of shorter reddish-grey hairs tipped with yellow. The eyes are large, black and prominent, the ears broad, open and rounded at the tips. Like all the other members of the family Mustelidae, the marten has special scent glands near the base of the tail. It is these which enable the skunk and the polecat to disgust their

enemies, but in the marten the secretion has a
musky odour and is not objectionable. In con-
sequence, one of its old English names was sweet-
mart to distinguish it from the foumart or polecat.

The pine marten is mainly arboreal, although in
Sutherland its chief habitat is open rocky ground.
The long slender body and sharp long claws
specially fit it for climbing whilst the long bushy tail
is useful as a balancer in negotiating slender
branches in the pursuit of birds, or in reaching their
nests for eggs. It is at least as agile in the trees as a
squirrel which it persistently kills; in destroying the
pine marten, the countryside was laid open to the
almost unrestricted spread of the grey squirrel.
Although so much at home in trees, the marten is at
times very active on the ground where it destroys

rats, mice, voles, rabbits, hares, gamebirds and domestic poultry, large and small. It is even accused of attacking lambs and stealing trout from fishing boats. It also eats caterpillars, beetles and carrion, and has a taste for bilberries, strawberries, cherries and raspberries, and even blackberries. It also robs beehives of their honey.

The female marten makes a nest of grass among the rocks, in a hollow tree, or utilizes an old crow's nest by relining it. She produces a single litter each year in late March or April of four or five, sometimes varied in number from two to seven, young. They are weaned at six to seven months and leave the nest soon after. They are easily tamed, though a captured adult is savage and untamable.

Martens are usually silent but use a high-pitched chattering in aggression and a deep huff as an alarm note. Mating is accompanied by purring and growling. The old spelling of the popular name was martin, but in recent works, to avoid any possible confusion with the birds of that name, zoologists have agreed to use 'e' as the second vowel.

The pine marten is found in all the wooded regions of Europe and in parts of Asia.

The Stoat

Family MUSTELIDAE *Mustela erminea*

Though the gun and the snare of the gamekeeper and the poultry-farmer have levied their toll upon the stoat as on the polecat, and the keeper's gibbet used always to show a row of stoats, the species is well represented, even in the strictly preserved woods of southern England, although today it is not commonly seen.

The stoat is up to 44 cm or more in length, of which about 11·4 cm make up the long-haired tail. Males are slightly larger than the females and weigh 200–440 g. The upper parts are red-brown and the underparts, white tinged with yellow. The tail is the same colour as the back, except that the tip is invariably a tuft of long black hairs. In the mountainous districts of Scotland, as in other northern countries of Europe, the fur in winter becomes pure white all over, with the exception of the tip of the tail which always remains black. This change takes place also in the north of England, but not so generally, and in the south it is only of rare occurrence, and often incomplete. Some parts remain brown, mainly on the head or back, or there may be no more than a ring around the eyes producing a spectacled appearance. The accepted idea is that the summer coat is 'protective' in that it harmonizes generally with the colour of the leaf litter and that, on snow-covered ground, the brown fur would make the animal conspicuous. This idea receives support from the fact that where snow is normal in winter, the stoat's coat changes to white. It is now thought, however, that the change in colour is partly dependent upon temperature (and the temperature of the previous winter at that) and partly upon the length of day. The change appears to be sudden but, in fact, this is because the new white coat grows underneath the old one before that is moulted in the autumn.

Like the polecat, the stoat can emit a most objectionable odour from its scent glands, but this is not quite so offensive as in the larger relative.

The stoat hunts largely by scent. It moves characteristically in a succession of low bounds in

*Stoat
in snow*

which the long, lithe body assumes an almost snake-like appearance. It can swim and climb well. Although the sense of smell is so acute, its hearing is also good but not its sight. Whether hunting or not, the stoat is alert, agile and energetic, with a natural ability to take advantage of cover. We have an indication of the effect of its manoeuvres on its living prey from the way a rabbit will cry in terror, apparently paralysed with fear, while the stoat is some way off. Under these circumstances a rabbit has been known to approach a group of men, apparently seeking refuge, even allowing itself to be picked up, its natural fear of man being not nearly so great as the terror inspired by the stoat. It is said that a hare, under similar circumstances, will not exert itself greatly to escape the stoat, but becomes so terrorized as to be unable to adopt methods with which it might outwit a fox or a pack of trained hounds.

Stoats also use 'charming' (see p. 64).

Stoats, truly carnivorous, reject little that is flesh. They hunt along the hedgerows, across fields, by rivers and brooks, or wherever there is a chance of food. All members of the weasel family readily take fish, and an eel or other fish placed in a trap is fairly certain bait for them. Where rabbits are common these are a frequent prey. Given the opportunity, a stoat can be destructive to game and poultry. The fact that the animal also destroys what is, in an agricultural sense, vermin is not so commonly stressed. It will, for example, destroy moles, as well as rats, although its prey is more usually the smaller rodents, such as mice and voles, killed by biting the back of the neck. It also takes small birds, eggs and reptiles.

Although largely nocturnal in its habits, it is not exclusively so, and there is more chance of seeing a stoat hunting in broad daylight than of seeing most of our native carnivores.

The nursery is made in a hole in a bank, or the hollow of a decayed tree. Here, about April or May, the female stoat gives birth to six to twelve young, which she alone looks after and which she will defend fiercely against all dangers. The babies have fine white hair covering the body at birth; the black tip appears on the tail at six to seven weeks and the eyes open at five to six weeks. The young are weaned at six weeks and remain with the mother for some time, the parents and offspring often hunting in a family party. It may be that two or more family parties join up to give the well-known stories of packs of stoats, which are said to attack a dog or even a man. There have also been occasions when, through increase in their numbers, the food supply of a district has been largely reduced and stoats have migrated in large numbers. There have been reports of several scores of them moving across country in a column.

The distribution of the stoat extends eastwards from Great Britain into Asia, and from the Alps and Pyrenees across Europe to its arctic shores.

A local race of smaller size, with some variation in the colouring—*M. e. hibernica*—is found in Ireland, and is there known as the weasel, but no specimens or skins of the true weasel (*M. nivalis*) have ever been received from that country. Another local race in the Isle of Jura, on the west coast of Scotland, is known as *M. e. ricinae*.

The Weasel

Family MUSTELIDAE   *Mustela nivalis*

Although of similar form to the stoat, the weasel is smaller and lacks the black tip to the tail. In colour there is little difference between the two except that the upper parts of the weasel are of a redder brown and the underparts a purer white, and the line of colours is less pronounced than in the stoat. The head is narrower and the legs are shorter, and the tail less bushy and little more than half the length of the stoat's tail. The average length of the adult male is 20 cm, with 6 cm of tail. The female is 2·5 cm or so less in total length than the male, and weighs, on average 59 g against his 115 g. Because of this smaller size, the females are known in some districts of England as cane weasels, under the impression that they represent a distinct species. There has also been the suggestion, which may have been influenced by the small size of the females, that we have another species in Britain, the least weasel (*Mustela rixosa*), but although this species extends from western Europe to eastern Asia and North America, it has not so far been found in this country.

The long slender body, short limbs, long neck and small head give the weasel a snake-like appearance, which is helped by its active gliding movements. In spite of its small size it will attack creatures larger than itself. It has been seen, in the neighbourhood of a barn, struggling to haul along a nearly full-grown rat two or three times its own weight, after it had killed it by biting through the base of the skull. Sometimes it hunts in couples, or in family packs.

Although the weasel is chiefly nocturnal it may also be active by day. Its diet includes rats, mice,

Weasel in typical attitude of rearing up and reconnoitring

voles, moles, frogs, small birds, eggs, rarely carrion, and occasionally it has killed poultry. It will swim in pursuit of the water vole, and will climb trees and bushes in order to rob a bird's nest of eggs or young. Voles and mice are probably its principal victims, its small size enabling it to pursue them in their underground runs.

The normal method of hunting is to stalk or trail prey but 'charming' is sometimes used (see also p. 64). The weasel's chief enemies, apart from man, are hawks and owls.

There is, as a rule, no seasonal change of colour in the weasel's fur in this country; but the occasional individual may be white or partially white in winter. The causes of the change appear to be the same as for the stoat (see p. 76).

The female weasel builds her nest in a hole in the bank or in some hollow tree. It consists of dry leaves, grass, moss and the like. From four to six—usually five—young are born in spring or early summer. The mother will defend them fearlessly. The young are weaned at four to five weeks and there is normally a second litter.

In Scotland the weasel has been known as the whittret, which is the equivalent of white-throat in Suffolk. In Yorkshire it is known as the ressel; in Cheshire, the mouse-killer; in Sussex, the beale; and in some parts of Surrey as kine, which suggests Gilbert White's cane, the local name in Hampshire for 'a little reddish beast not much bigger than a field-mouse but much longer,' of his fifteenth letter to Pennant. The more general name weasel is the Anglo-Saxon wesle.

When Scotland suffered severely from a plague of field voles in 1892, the Board of Agriculture appointed a Committee of Enquiry, and the examination of witnesses—farmers, keepers, shepherds— clearly established the fact that the chief natural enemy of the field vole is the weasel, and that the gravest mistake had been made in destroying such

82

large numbers. It was even suggested that weasels should be imported from the Continent and turned loose.

The voice is a guttural hiss when alarmed and a short screaming bark when disturbed, but neither is heard at all commonly.

The weasel is found throughout Britain, but is absent from most islands, and from Ireland.

The American Mink

Family MUSTELIDAE *Mustela vison*

The rearing of mink on farms was established in Britain in 1929. Inevitably some animals escaped into the wild but there were no records of them breeding until 1957, when young mink were seen on

American mink

the River Teign in Devon. Since then there have been widespread reports of breeding in England, Wales, Scotland, and Ireland, despite attempts to control their numbers by trapping, because they prey on poultry, pheasants, water fowl and domestic rabbits as well as wild birds and mammals. They will also take trout and crayfish.

The mink is similar in form to the stoat but usually larger and with a longer tail. Typically the fur is uniformly dark brown with a white throat-patch, but colour varieties have been established by artificial selection. It is a solitary, nocturnal animal, each one having a den in a cleft of rock or perhaps an enlarged water vole hole. Five to six young are born in the spring. Up to 17 pound.

The Polecat

Family MUSTELIDAE   *Mustela putorius*

In contrast to the sweet-mart or pine marten, the polecat was named the foumart or foul marten, because the secretion from the glands under the tail is intolerably acrid and has an appalling smell. On this account the fur is considered by some to be useless, but it was extensively used in the early nineteenth century, and to a slight extent today. Like the marten, the polecat, thanks mainly to the gin-trap and persecution by the gamekeeper, has become very rare in this country whereas formerly it was widespread. It is now found only in Wales and a few adjoining counties, and in Wales its numbers seem to be increasing. It is still common throughout Europe.

Although in general appearance similar to the marten, the polecat is smaller, has shorter legs and a shorter tail, and differs in colour. Male polecats measure, on average, 52 cm, from nose tip to tail tip, whilst females measure slightly less, 46 cm. The average weight of males is 987 g, that of females 623 g. The long coarse fur is dark brown on the upper parts with dense yellowish underfur showing through, and black on the underparts. The legs and tail are black, as is the head, which has white markings on the ears, on the chin extending on to the muzzle and on the cheeks. In winter these markings tend to join over the eyes and, rarely, to join up with the chin patch.

Its usual habitat is a wood or copse, not too far from a plunderable farm; but it has no fixed type of

Polecat

dwelling, taking advantage of any hole such as a fox-earth, a rabbit burrow, or a natural rock crevice; often a woodstack in the farmyard has been used. With the approach of winter, polecats may seek shelter in deserted buildings. The polecat is less agile than the marten and less of a climber. It is active mainly at night.

The polecat has always shared with the stoat and weasel the reputation of a wanton killer of domestic poultry and there is no doubt this reputation has sometimes been deserved. But it is predators such as the polecat that keep the populations of small mammals, especially rats and mice, within bounds. It eats a wide variety of prey including rats, mice, voles, hedgehogs and rabbits. Eggs, birds, frogs and lizards are also taken, as well as some insect food. Its usual method of carrying smaller prey is to grip them by the middle of the back, much as a retriever carries game. There has been one record of the discovery in the larder of a polecat bitch in addition to the remains of rats, mice, rabbits, birds and eels, of the bodies of three kittens which were known to have been drowned at least 402 m away.

Mating occurs in April and it seems likely there is only one litter a year in about June, consisting of three to eight, but usually five to six young. They have a thin covering of white hair when first born, the colours and markings of the adults appearing by the age of fifty days.

Polecats are usually silent, but are said to use occasional short yelps, clucks and chatterings.

Family MUSTELIDAE   **The Polecat Ferret**
This animal has been the cause of perplexity on two counts; firstly because it has sometimes given rise to

stories of pine martens seen far from where they now live and secondly because there is some doubt about its origin. The truth seems to be that breeders have back-crossed ferrets, which are domesticated albino polecats, with the wild polecat.

The ferret was known to the Romans as a domesticated animal and is believed to be an albino strain of the Asiatic polecat. They may have introduced it to Britain. Certainly ferrets have been used in this country for centuries. The name itself dates from the mid-fifteenth century, when the animal was used for driving out rats and rabbits. Throughout that time innumerable ferrets have escaped and interbred with the wild polecats.

A fully-coloured polecat-ferret is usually smaller, on the whole a lighter colour than the wild polecat, and often skewbald, with more or less large patches of white on the usual polecat colours.

No species name is given for the polecat ferret because if it is a cross between a polecat and a ferret, it is a hybrid between two species.

The Wild Cat

Family FELIDAE   *Felis silvestris grampia*

The wild cat exists today mainly in the rocky parts of northern Scotland, north of the Great Glen. It is said to have increased considerably in numbers there, in recent years and is spreading south.

It inhabits the most lonely and inaccessible mountainsides, hiding during the day among rocks, prowling far and wide at night in search of prey. It is of a general yellowish grey colour, but there is a good deal of variation. Individuals differ in their dark brown markings, some having vertical stripes

87

running down the sides; in others these are broken up to form spots.

Since there seems to have been considerable cross-breeding with feral domestic cats, some of the variation in the pattern of the coat may be due to this. The wild cat has a squarish thick head and a stouter and longer body than the domestic cat, but the thick bushy tail is relatively shorter, ringed, and ending in a long black tip. The limbs, too, are longer than those of the tame cat, so that the wild cat stands higher. The fur is long, soft and thick. The average length is about 84 cm of which the tail accounts for 28 cm, but there is a record of a Scottish example measuring 1·14 m in all. The weight of a male averages 5 kg, but may be as much as 6·8 kg, and that of the female 3·8 kg, with a maximum of 4·5 kg. One wild cat from the Carpathians weighed nearly 15 kg.

This animal is the fiercest and most destructive beast we have. Its strength and ferocity when hard pressed are perfectly astonishing. The wild and unearthly cry of the wild cat echoes far in the quiet night.

The female makes a nest in some remote rock-cleft or hollow tree, away from the male who may kill the kittens. There are two breeding seasons in a year, in early March and again in late May or early June, the litters of four to five kittens being born in May and August respectively. Occasionally a third litter has been recorded in December or January, but these may have been from a domestic–wild cat cross. The kittens have a light ground colour with greyish-brown tabby markings. They leave the nest at four to five weeks old but do not go hunting with the mother until ten to twelve weeks old. They are

Scottish wild cat

not weaned until the age of four months, and leave the mother at five months old.

The voice is meeow, a growl when angry and a purr when pleased, with the typical small cat scream or caterwaul on occasions.

The distribution of the wild cat, of which the Scottish wild cat is a subspecies, includes Europe and Northern Asia to the north Himalayas. Although formerly widespread over the whole of Britain, and at one time a beast of chase in England, it appears never to have been a native of Ireland.

The Rabbit

Family LEPORIDAE   *Oryctolagus cuniculus*

It is fairly certain that it was the Normans who introduced the rabbit here. The name 'rabbit' is from the French, and originally indicated the suckling young, the adults being known as conies.

The ears of the rabbit are remarkably long. The eyes are large and prominent, and placed well to the sides of the head. The hindlegs are longer than the forelegs, and instead of pads on the soles protecting the feet, all Leporidae have a thick coating of hair which gives a firm grip either on hard rock or slippery snow. The tail is very short and turned up. The fur is of triple formation; there is a dense, soft, woolly underfur, through which project the longer and stronger hairs which give the coat its colour, and a still longer but much less numerous set, scattered among the others. The two longer sorts of hair are more or less ringed. The coat becomes thicker in winter. Its colour varies considerably but it is usually greyish-buff sprinkled with black. The nape is reddish and the underparts whitish. The tail is black above and white below.

Rabbits are sexually mature at a very early age. The females have longer and more delicately modelled heads than bucks which are slightly larger than does and may be up to 41 cm long, head and body, and weigh up to 4 kg.

Rabbits are not promiscuous, as was thought, but polygamous, one buck mating with several does, each doe keeping to her own territory within the warren, and the old bucks driving away all young bucks.

The rabbit is not specially built for burrowing,

yet, where the soil is light, the combined efforts of many generations have resulted in an extensive and complicated system of burrows, with bolt-runs as emergency exits and stop-runs for nursery use. Although it prefers the light sand of the dunes or a sandy heath, it has been known to burrow deeply into dry clay or even a surface seam of coal. The forepaws are principally used in burrowing, the loosened earth being thrown back by the kicking of the hind feet. Where stones come in the way and cannot be loosened by the paws, they have been known to be removed by the teeth. Typical tunnels are about 15 cm in diameter, increased at points along their length to 30 cm, to provide passing places. The residential quarters are always blind chambers leading from the main passages. Adult rabbits use no bedding materials but rest on the bare soil. The pregnant doe, however, makes a bed for her young of hay or straw, lined with fur stripped from her underparts.

Litters of rabbits succeed one another rapidly at intervals of about a month from January to June, but there is some sporadic breeding in the other months of the year. The young are usually born in a 'stab' or 'stop', a short burrow about 60 cm long, just under the surface, usually well away from the main burrow to avoid the danger of the buck killing them. The litters vary from two to eight, the higher numbers being those of the warmer months. Newly born rabbits are blind and deaf, their ears being closed. They are almost naked, and have no power of movement until about the tenth day. The eyes open at seven days and at 18 days they can run and make short excursions from the underground nest. Before they are a month old they are capable of independent existence. The young are full-grown at nine months old but sexual maturity is reached in three to four months.

Rabbits are normally silent, except for occasional low growls and grunts, or, when terrorized by a stoat, the rabbit utters a loud scream. A doe has also been heard to utter low notes when nursing her young. Another sound used more deliberately is a thump on the ground with both hindfeet together. This is an alarm signal, usually given by an old buck, to which all rabbits within earshot respond by dash-

European rabbit

ing towards their burrows. Their main enemies are members of the weasel family, fox and badger, owls and hawks.

The chief food is grass, but rabbits can devastate crops and inflict serious loss on the farmer. The exception to a vegetable diet is found in its occasional indulgence in snails and earthworms.

In 1954 and 1955, an introduced disease, known as myxomatosis, made the wild rabbit a rare animal. The disease has now declined and there are signs of the rabbit recovering. However, as soon as numbers begin to build up in any locality, the disease seems to take its toll again. There have been reports from this country and from Australia of rabbits' nests, with young on the surface. Surface nesting became pronounced soon after myxomatosis struck the rabbit here, and one view put forward was that non-burrowing individuals may have been less prone to the disease. By their multiplication, a population was produced with a high ratio of surface nesters.

The Brown Hare

Family LEPORIDAE   *Lepus capensis*

Although similar in general form and structure to the closely related rabbit, the hare differs in having a longer body, longer hind limbs, longer ears with their invariable black tips, and tawny fur on the upper parts. In addition, while the rabbit is gregarious, the hare is usually solitary.

The total length of the hare is about 61 cm. The weight averages about 4 kg. The shoulders, neck and flanks are of a ruddier hue than the back, which is a mixture of grey and brown. The underside is pure white except at the breast and loins where the ruddy tint is continued from above. There is a profusion of black and white whiskers, of which the white are the longer. The tail, which is carried curved up over the back or straight behind, is black above and white on the sides and below. The large, prominent eyes have a horizontal pupil and their situation well to the sides of the head affords a wide field of vision. The male, or jack, has a smaller body, shorter head, and redder shoulders than the doe.

The hare does not burrow and does not seek refuge underground from its enemies, unless hard pressed, when it may enter a rabbit burrow temporarily. Instead, it relies for security on speed, or upon crouching in the low vegetation where its russet coat harmonizes generally with its surroundings.

The resting-place is a slight depression in the long grass known as a 'form', where the hare crouches during the day, always alert and ready to use its superior speed to escape if disturbed.

At dusk it goes abroad to feed, and returns to the form at dawn. To break the continuity of scent, when it is leaving its form, and again when returning to it, it will suddenly turn at right angles to its former course and make a prodigious leap—4·5 m or more—to the top of a bank. It will then take another long bound, perhaps into marshy ground where the scent will not lie, and from there to the feeding-ground proper. Another tactic frequently employed is that of doubling on its tracks. The hare is a good swimmer, and often crosses rivers and streams in order to reach a better feeding-ground, to avoid pursuit, or to seek a mate. It has been known to cross a river 183 m wide in order to reach a field of carrots on the other side.

Brown hare in marshy habitat in early spring

The 'form' is usually made in rank grass among thickets of gorse and briar, or in the open field where the ground is dry beneath it. It takes and retains the shape of the animal's body, and the same form may be used for a long period. Here the doe brings forth her litter of two, three or four young—occasionally more. The leverets are born with their eyes open, and a short furry coat, which lacks the ruddiness of the adult. They are capable of using their limbs within a very short time of birth, and each is sufficiently well advanced at birth to be able to occupy its own form near that of the mother. The doe visits each in turn to suckle them and will fight desperately in their defence. They are quite independent at a month old.

The adults pair promiscuously and have several

litters a year as they appear to be capable of breeding all the year round, with a peak in spring and summer.

The hare is exclusively vegetarian, its diet including bark, grain and roots, as well as herbaceous plants. It is very destructive to young trees in plantations, and where hares are numerous the farmer and market-gardener suffer severely from its depredations among the crops of carrot, lettuce, turnip and other vegetables. In the open country it prefers grasses, clover, sow-thistle and chicory. When it gets into gardens it shows distinct preference for dahlias, carnations, pinks, nasturtiums, parsley and thyme. In shrubberies it is very destructive to bark and boughs, especially of coniferous trees.

The proverbial expression 'Mad as a March hare' has reference to the insane antics of the jack hares during the rutting season. In spring they lose much of their customary caution and assemble in groups,

Brown hare leverets eight days old

the males fighting and chasing the females. The antics of the males include bucking on stiff legs, kicking and stand-up boxing-matches between rivals. In bucking one may leap over his opponent and kick him vigorously with the hind feet. When wounded or badly frightened he utters a scream like that of a child in pain. Hares have also a warning sound made by grinding the teeth, which appears to be passed on from hare to hare, having the same result as the stamping of the hindfeet by the rabbit. The courtship notes of buck and doe are different, and their imitation by poachers and gamekeepers is known as hare-sucking.

The brown hare is widely distributed in England, Wales and Scotland up to about 600 m, except in Scotland where the blue hare *L. timidus scoticus* replaces it from 300 m upwards. It is not a native of Ireland, which has instead a subspecies of *L. timidus*, known as the Irish hare.

The Scottish Hare

Family LEPORIDAE   *Lepus timidus scoticus*

The Scottish hare is regarded as a subspecies of *L. timidus* of Scandinavia and the Alps. Known also as the blue or variable hare, it is indigenous only in Scotland but it has been introduced into some of the neighbouring isles, and also into northern England, north Wales and Northern Ireland.

The name variable hare denotes its change of colour at the beginning of winter after the manner of the stoat. In Cheshire it is known as the white hare. It used to be thought that the winter whitening of the fur was, like the senile whitening of human hair, due to the activity of certain wandering cells, which removed the pigment. The probability is that a process takes place similar to that seen in the stoat and weasel, which has been more fully investigated (see pp. 76, 82). It is noteworthy that the black tips of the ears, like the black tip of the tail of the stoat, never change colour. Moreover, the outer half of the ear below the black tip remains brown, and there is always an area of grey, of variable size, on the back. The Scottish hare is smaller than the brown hare, the combined length of head and body being about 51 cm, but the head is proportionately larger, the ears and tail shorter, and the legs longer. The weight is about 3·5 kg in fully grown individuals. The fur is more woolly and of a greyer tint in summer—giving a 'blue' appearance—the whiskers shorter and finer, the eyes rounder, and the hair on the underside of the foot softer. Behind the breast the underparts are white, and the tail wholly so.

The habits of the Scottish hare are very similar to those of the brown hare, except that, instead of making a form, it lies up in rock crevices and among stones, usually above the line of cultivation, where it may be sheltered from the sight of birds of prey overhead. In general its food is similar, but it is said to feed on lichens in winter. The breeding habits do not appear to differ greatly from those of the brown hare. Breeding begins in February, reaches a peak in March and falls off in July. Two or three litters are produced in a year, and the leverets vary in number up to eight.

The Irish Hare

Family LEPORIDAE   *Lepus timidus hibernicus*

The Irish hare occurs all over Ireland, and is not

found elsewhere except in north Wales and the Island of Mull, where attempts have been made to introduce it.

Although it is larger than the Scottish hare, there is a tendency today to identify the Irish hare completely with the Scottish hare and to ignore the subspecific names. The head and body average about 58 cm in length, and the tail about 9 cm. The ears slightly exceed the tail in length. The average weight is about 3 kg. It has russet fur, not smoky brown as in the Scottish hare. The winter whitening is not regular as in that subspecies, and is frequently only patchy, russet 'islands' being left surrounded by white. As compared with the brown hare, the Irish hare is smaller and of more graceful build, but the head is relatively longer and broader, the eyes rounder, the ears shorter and the limbs longer.

The Red Squirrel

Family SCIURIDAE   *Sciurus vulgaris leucourus*

The red squirrel is one of the most attractive of our small mammals, especially when it is sitting on its haunches on a branch, its feathered tail curled up its back, its tufted ears erect, and its forepaws holding a nut; or when leaping with characteristic grace from bough to bough.

From the end of the snout to the tip of the tail proper, that is excluding the hairs that extend beyond the tip, it measures only about 39 cm and of this nearly half is tail. Weight ranges from 260–345 g. It is customary to speak of the tail as bushy. Rather it should be described as feathered, the hairs extending outwards and backwards on each side. The muzzle is well furnished with whiskers, the prominent eyes are black and bright, and the large, pointed ears bear tufts of long hairs in winter. The hindlimbs are much longer than the forelimbs, and the heel of the long hindfoot is planted on the surface of the bough when the squirrel is at rest. The feet are well adapted for climbing. The forefeet have four fingers and a rudimentary thumb, and the hindfeet have five toes. The soles are hairy, and the long curved claws are needle-sharp. The upper parts and tail are brownish red and the underparts white. Before winter, when the fur becomes softer and thicker, a grey tinge is developed on the sides, and the ear-tufts become longer and bushy; these are shed in the breeding season. The tail may have a creamy tint in summer.

The red squirrel is diurnal, with peaks of activity in the early morning and just before dusk. It does not hibernate. In the winter it may sleep more than in the summer, but it is still active, even during cold weather. It is an expert swimmer, although it only takes to water deliberately in exceptional circumstances. The voice is a rasping chatter followed by a hoarse call or whine. The young have a shrill piping call.

The red squirrel builds nests in the branches of trees, not merely as nurseries, but also for shelter and sleep. There may be several of these in adjacent trees and some may be crows' or magpies' nests converted by the new tenants; usually they are the squirrel's own work. They are bulky structures composed of twigs, strips of thin bark, moss, and leaves; some are cup-shaped, others domed. These are usually known as 'dreys'. The breeding nest is a huge ball of sticks and leaves, sometimes made in a roomy hollow in a tree trunk. The breeding period

Red squirrel

largely depends on the quantity of food available and on weather conditions. Typically there are two main seasons in the south, January to April and late May to August, but apparently only one in Scotland. Litters may contain one to six young, the usual being three or four, born blind and naked. They remain with their parents until they themselves are adult.

The food of the red squirrel is fairly varied. In pine woods the cones provide the staple food and the ground beneath a squirrel's tree will be found littered with chips and cores of the cone from which the seeds have been extracted. In beech woods they feed largely on mast, the sharp-edged triangular seeds contained in the prickly beechnuts.

Hazel nuts are a favourite food for storing in considerable quantities in holes in the ground. Wild cherries are also taken. An item in a squirrel's diet which perhaps results in the most damage is the bark taken from the leader-shoots of young pines, thereby deforming the trees. This is off-set, to some extent, by its feeding on the larvae of the pine tortrix moth which burrow in the tips of the young pine shoots. It also takes bird's eggs and nestlings. It will also come down on the ground and feed on strawberries, bilberries and fungi.

In former times the red squirrel was wantonly persecuted, squirrel hunts being a popular sport in areas where it is no longer found. It was formerly distributed throughout Great Britain and Ireland, wherever there was sufficient woodland, but it is now absent from the Isle of Man and absent or, at best, scarce in the south-eastern counties of England and in a large part of the Midlands, its main stronghold being East Anglia. It is now abundant in Scotland in only a few areas. Outside Britain, it extends across Europe, from the tree line southwards to the Mediterranean, and into Asia.

The Grey Squirrel

Family SCIURIDAE   *Sciurus carolinensis*

The grey squirrel is a native of eastern North America, introduced into the British Isles as a pet in the nineteenth century and now persecuted as a pest. It had been liberated in various parts of the country at different times, but made no spectacular progress until the beginning of World War I when it spread from Woburn Park, Bedfordshire, into Buckinghamshire and Hertfordshire. Now the grey squirrel is established along the south coast, from Kent to Dorset and Cornwall, and northwards to the Scottish border. It appears to be absent from the Isle of Wight, Anglesey and the Isle of Man, and also Cumberland, and there are only sporadic records for Norfolk, Caernarvonshire, Westmorland and Northumberland. There are areas of infestation in eight counties of Scotland, and some introductions into Ireland.

Larger than the red squirrel, it is a speckled grey above and white on the underparts, the head and body measuring nearly 30 cm, the tail 20–24 cm. Its weight is 510–570 g. Apart from slight tufts in winter, it lacks the pronounced ear-tufts of the red squirrel and the tail is markedly less bushy. Its habits are similar to those of the red squirrel except that it is more aggressive and it frequents open woodlands and parklands rather than the coniferous woods, one result of which is that it is not found in such high altitudes as the red squirrel.

Reports of red squirrels seen in areas where only

grey squirrels are known to be are not infrequent. Changes in the coat in both species throughout the year, cause some confusion. Red squirrels have more grey in winter and grey squirrels more chestnut in summer. There is also the complication of the grey

Grey squirrel

having ear-tufts in winter. Nevertheless, there should be no mistaking the red, particularly in its winter dress, because of the very pronounced ear-tufts.

In addition to acorns, nuts and beech mast, grey squirrels eat a variety of things. They eat toadstools, as well as the *Boletus*, and they will eat puff-balls, not infrequently burying these fungi. They will tear oak galls to pieces, presumably to eat the insect larvae. Squirrels will sometimes, for no apparent reason, chew to pieces the lead labels naming the trees, or take to biting off whole leaves of horse-chestnuts. They will take the inner layers of the bark of sycamore and beech presumably for the sugars, or strip bark from the dead twigs of limes to line their nests. They will also eat the green buds of young trees. It is for these reasons that grey squirrels are so unpopular with foresters.

Nuts, acorns and other foods are buried singly in the ground and well spread out. When winter comes the buried food is found by scent, even when the ground is covered by snow, so that an individual may not necessarily return to the nut or acorn it has buried but all squirrels in the locality share the cached foods. Often the food may be carried some distance.

During the pre-mating period several males may chase one female. The sound made by males chasing females is said to be low and vibrating like the song of a grasshopper. Grey squirrels also use many variations of purring (when feeding), chattering, scolding and barking.

Two kinds of nest are made. One is the winter drey, also used for a nursery. It is of leafy twigs, domed and usually in the angle between a branch and the trunk. It is lined with leaves, bark, moss or grass and especially honeysuckle bark. The summer drey is a leafy platform built out on the branches.

The breeding season lasts from the end of December until June. There are two litters a year, of one to seven young, but the usual number is three, naked and blind at birth. Weaned at seven to ten weeks, the young reach adult size at eight months and are sexually mature at six to eleven months.

Grey squirrels swim well but there are signs that the spread of grey squirrels in Britain is controlled by rivers. It may be, therefore, that a few individuals take far more readily to the water than the rest.

It is often said that the grey squirrel ousted the red in Britain but the latter appears to have been decimated by a disease at about the time that the grey squirrel started to spread. Some years ago a campaign for the total extermination of the grey squirrel was undertaken. It is now known to have had little effect, largely due to the grey squirrels' ability to keep out of sight among the trees.

The Dormouse

Family GLIRIDAE   *Muscardinus avellanarius*

The dormouse looks like a miniature squirrel with the same shaped head, prominent black eyes, large ears and thickly furred tail, as well as in its arboreal habitat and its habit of sitting up on its haunches and holding a nut or other food in its forepaws. However, in its anatomy it shows a closer affinity to mice.

The total length of the dormouse is about 14 cm, of which nearly half is tail. The weight is variable, from 23–43 g, being greatest just before hibernation. The forelimbs, which are much shorter than the hindlimbs, have four separate fingers and a rudimentary thumb, while the hind-feet have five toes, of which one is vestigial. All the claws are short, and on the underside of each foot there are six large pads. The fur of the upper parts is light tawny, that of the underside yellowish white, but the throat and adjoining part of the chest is a purer white. The head is comparatively large, with blunt muzzle, prominent eyes, broadly rounded short ears, and long whiskers.

The dormouse can be found in the copse, the thick hedgerow, scrub and secondary growth in woods, where there are trees such as hazel and beech with edible seeds. It seems to be almost wholly nocturnal, although it can occasionally be seen about in the daytime. The daily sleep approaches the deep sleep of hibernation, with a heavy fall in the body-temperature and in the rate of breathing, so that the animal gives the appearance of being actually dead. It is not a case of 'sleeping with one eye open' with the dormouse. It needs to be shaken to arouse it.

Three to five globular sleeping nests are built in a season of twigs, moss and grass, about 76 mm in diameter, and sometimes with a round opening. Although they may be sited among the stubs of a coppice or beneath a tussock of grass, they are typically suspended high up in the bushes. The nursery nest is twice this size. In some districts the nest will be constructed of the bark of old honey-suckle stems, shredded into ribbons. The inner lining is of the same material more finely divided, with a bed of leaves.

The female drives the male away from the nursery nest, to occupy a sleeping nest on his own. There appear to be one or two litters of three or four, or even six or seven, blind and naked young born in spring or summer, but there are also records of young being found in September or October. It is probable that, as these are born so near to the period of hibernation, they do not survive as they would not be able to provide their own shelter or go without food for a long period. However, their survival cannot be ruled out as impossible. The first coat which the young acquire by the age of 13 days, is more grey than red but after moulting they gradually assume the adult coat. Their eyes open at 18 days, and the animals start to forage. They become independent in 40 days or less.

Hibernation is from late October until April, each individual hibernating on its own. During the period preceding this there is an accumulation of fat in the body, and further provision for the winter is made by laying up a store of nuts. The winter sleep is not continuous; the dormouse wakes at intervals for a meal, and then goes to sleep again. The winter nest is usually under moss at the base of a tree or in a hedge-bottom, commonly under dry leaves, or occasionally far underground. The onset of hibernation appears to be influenced by temperature and other atmospheric conditions, and possibly also by the accumulation of fat. In hibernation the dormouse rolls itself into a ball. Its temperature drops so low that the body feels cold. The pulse is slow and feeble and the muscles are held rigid.

The food is much the same as that of a squirrel but it is particularly fond of the hazel-nut, a good fat producer, beech mast and chestnut, pine seeds, haws, young shoots and bark. It does not crack the shell of the nut, but gnaws quite a small hole in it. In

Common dormouse

addition it may eat insects and has been said sometimes to take birds' eggs or even young birds.

The dormouse used to be a favourite pet, largely
because it is gentle and shows little disposition to
bite, but it seems to be more rare now, perhaps the
result of competition for food with the grey squirrel.
There is a high mortality in winter when it falls prey
to magpies and carrion crows, foxes, badgers, stoats,
weasels and rats, possibly also grey squirrels. Four
out of five dormice, it has been estimated, are killed
during hibernation.

In Europe the dormouse is found no farther north
than Sweden and it does not occur in Scotland. It is
absent from Ireland. In England it is found mainly
in the south and west, being absent from East Anglia

and infrequent in the Midlands. In Wales it is scarce and somewhat local. Outside Europe it extends only to Asia Minor. The English name can be traced back certainly to the fifteenth century, and is considered to embody the verb dorm = to doze.

The Edible, Fat or Squirrel-tailed Dormouse

Family GLIRIDAE   *Glis glis*

Although the consumption of dormice is now prohibited by law, the edible dormouse was once thought of as a great table delicacy by the Romans, hence its common name. It is the largest of the European dormice with a total length of 36 cm. Its fur is short, thick and silvery or brownish grey, with a ring of black fur around the eyes making them appear very large. The bushy tail, which is as long as the rest of the body, and the grey fur sometimes cause confusion with the grey squirrel, but the dormouse is smaller and is nocturnal.

Normally inhabitants of deciduous woodland where they live on fruit, nuts, insects and bark, edible dormice often invade houses where they seek places to hibernate. Prior to hibernation in October weight is increased, but there will be up to 50% loss of body weight by the time they wake in April. Breeding starts in mid-June with one litter of two to seven young, in a nest in a tree-hole.

The edible dormouse was first introduced into England in 1902 when Walter Rothschild released some in Tring Park. Until 1963 its range was within a triangle bounded by Beaconsfield, Aylesbury and Luton, where they appeared to do little damage. In

1963, however, the dormice were found to be causing extensive damage on a Forestry Commission estate at Wendover. Damage to conifers, especially spruce, was sometimes causing the tops of the trees to die. (Illustration p. 112.)

The Bank Vole

Family CRICETIDAE   *Clethrionomys glareolus*

There can be little doubt that in many places the bank vole has been mistaken for a bright variation of the field vole. Its habits are much the same, except that it haunts the hedgerow and wooded country rather than the open fields. Its head and body length is 8·8–10·1 cm, the tail being nearly half this length and ending in a pencil of hairs. The ears and feet are proportionately large, the former also being more oval than round. The bank vole differs from the other voles in the fact that the molar teeth become rooted in the jaws of the adults.

The fur of the upper parts is a bright chestnut-red or vandyke brown, except the hairy tail, which is black above. The underparts, including the lower side of the tail, are whitish varying to yellowish or even buff. The redder tint causes this species sometimes to be referred to as the red vole. It has pink lips, and grey feet, and its whiskers are about 25 mm long. Black and albino varieties have been recorded.

The bank vole is much more agile than the short-tailed vole but less given to jumping or burrowing. It may be seen in sunny situations at any time of the day, preferring warm, dry places, but it is also found in wet places. It is a good swimmer and diver. It constructs shallow runs in the earth of a roadside bank or hedgebank. These have many entrances and

Bank vole attracted to an apple

Edible or fat dormouse

exits at different levels, some of the passages connecting it with the top of the bank others enlarging into blind chambers. Its food includes herbage, roots, bulbs, fruits and seeds; it appears to be particularly fond of turnips. In spring it has been observed climbing rose and hawthorn bushes in order to nibble the new leaves, and in autumn to obtain the hips and haws. It also eats nuts, berries, the grain of wheat and barley, and the seeds of smaller grasses. Insects and larvae make up about a third of its food, and snails, and even small birds are eaten. It has been known to eat the unpalatable shrew it has killed. In Scotland it is suspected of eating the shoot-buds of young conifers, especially of larch, and gnawing the bark from branches. In Britain it is occasionally caught in the act of robbing household stores, but in more northern regions, as in Norway, it is a constant inhabitant of houses. It does not hibernate and therefore, as a rule, does not lay up food stores. It is markedly diurnal in thick cover, but probably has alternating periods of activity and sleep throughout each twenty-four hours. It is said to be more active at night in summer.

The breeding season starts at the middle of April, rises to a peak in June, then declines in intensity until October, but there may be a limited amount of breeding in all months between October and April. The males appear quarrelsome and when fighting or pairing are very vocal, indulging in grunting squeaks. There are several litters of three to six, or more, naked and blind young during the year, produced in nests of grass, moss and wool, or feathers, usually placed above ground, sometimes in a bird's nest at a fair height. The young are weaned at two and a half weeks.

It appears to be widely distributed, and to occur over the whole of mainland Scotland; but it is not recorded from the Isle of Man, Hebrides, or Shetland. Recorded from Ireland from 1964.

The Water Vole

Family CRICETIDAE   *Arvicola terrestris*

The water vole, a comparatively inoffensive rodent, is apt to suffer from its folk name 'water rat', although it is not a rat or of a rat-like nature.

It has the characteristics of a vole: a short thick head with the muzzle rounded instead of being pointed; the limbs relatively short; the eyes small and extremely short-sighted; and the small, round ears scarcely projecting beyond the surrounding fur. The feet are naked and pale pink beneath, with five rounded pads, and clothed with stiff hairs on the upper surface. The thick, long, glossy fur may be of a warm reddish-brown above, sprinkled with grey but it is commonly a blackish-grey. On the underparts it is yellowish-grey. The female is slightly smaller than the male and more greyish-brown. The head and body measure 19–22 cm, the tapering and hairy ringed tail is about 12 cm. Weight varies from 120–180 g in winter to almost double this in summer.

The water vole does not hibernate, but it has been said to lay up considerable stores for times when food is scarce and difficult to find. These stores consist of nuts, beech mast, acorns, and the creeping underground stems of the horsetails. Water voles have been reported eating caddis-worms and other insects and they take freshwater snails and mussels. Apart from these their food is mainly vegetable:

Water vole on river bank

succulent grasses, flags, loosestrife, sedges and other riverside plants.

It appears to have a four-hourly rhythm of activity throughout the day and night, with feeding periods of about half an hour alternating with periods of rest or random movement. Opinions, however, differ on this. It is sometimes found in fields far away from any water. Paradoxically, the water vole remains within its burrow, or does not go far afield, during heavy rain.

The loud sudden 'plop' as it drops into the water is the observer's first intimation of the presence of a water vole. We may occasionally track its course under water, but as a rule it at once disappears, and surfaces some distance away or retreats into its burrow in the bank, sometimes by an underwater entrance, or regains the bank by an upper exit. It is a steady swimmer, but it is less skilful in swimming than in diving.

The burrows have been said to cause considerable damage to the dykes in Fenland, and where ponds have been constructed by artificial banking. Otherwise, the water vole is largely inoffensive.

The breeding season lasts from early April to October. The female makes a thick-walled globular nest of reeds and grasses in a chamber under the bank, or in a hollow willow or even in a bird's nest for her litter of about five (two to seven) naked and blind young. The number of litters in a season is not known for certain, but the young of early litters mature quickly and may breed before winter. The water vole has many enemies especially when young. Its life-span is little more than a year in the wild.

The water vole is generally distributed in Britain, but does not occur in Ireland or the Scottish islands. Two subspecies have been recorded in Yorkshire and Scotland north of the Clyde, respectively, but as *A. terrestris* is variable throughout its range too much emphasis cannot be placed on these supposed subspecies.

The Short-tailed Vole

Family CRICETIDAE   *Microtus agrestis*

The short-tailed vole has been called the grass mouse, field mouse or field vole. The general stumpy form with the blunt oval outline of the head, the short, round ears just protruding from the reddish-brown fur of the upper parts and the short, rather stiff tail, are points sufficient to distinguish it from any of our mice. On the underside the fur is

Field or meadow vole, also known as short-tailed vole

greyish-white. The hind feet have six pads on the under surface, as compared with the five of the water vole. The length of head and body is 9–12 cm, the tail being a third of the body length. The weight varies from 20–40 g.

The typical habitat of the short-tailed vole in-includes meadows and damp pastures, but it will also be found in gardens, orchards and plantations. In such places it does enormous damage, its food being almost entirely the hard stem and leaves of grasses, although it will nibble almost anything vegetable, including bark. It must, however, be placed to its credit that it catches and consumes large numbers of insects, among them the destructive larch sawfly. In its underground burrows it lays up extensive stores of food for the winter, but it is not correct to say that the underground burrows include its summer nest. These burrows connect with a network of above-ground runs through the grass and herbage, with occasional holes enabling the vole to bolt underground. These surface runs are made without disturbing the grass blades, which cross above them and so enable the vole to run or creep along them without being seen by a hawk circling high overhead. It is less successful in eluding the owl, which hunts much nearer to the ground, and the weasel which can follow it into its runs. Other enemies include the kestrel, buzzard and foxes.

The female vole makes her nest beside a rank tuft of grass along one of the surface runs. It is roofed with a dome of grass blades divided longitudinally, and plaited and felted. There is nothing to distinguish it from its surroundings, so that only a trained eye would see it. It may be detected by the finer character (due to shredding) of the grass. The female enters or emerges from any point under the edge of the dome, and if the nest is uncovered suddenly she will at once bolt, leaving her youngsters unprotected. Characteristically, when the nest is disturbed, the most we see of the mother is a shape which flashes away and disappears into the adjacent grass.

The breeding season lasts from February to September. Like all our rodents the young are naked and blind, at birth. There may be five, six or seven in a litter, with several litters in a season. The young are weaned at fourteen to twenty-eight days and mate at six weeks of age.

In districts where weasels and owls, as well as other predators, have been more or less exterminated, the natural increases of the short-tailed vole are allowed full play, and they can become a plague. Crops have been cleared from the fields, young trees in plantations destroyed by the thousand, and even newly-sown cornfields rendered unproductive because every seedling has been eaten. In the New Forest and the Forest of Dean great loss has been sustained at various times by the voles severing the roots of young trees that crossed their runs, and by gnawing the bark of the young trunks. The most effective of the plans adopted for lessening their numbers was by sinking pits 45 cm deep, wider at the bottom than at the mouth, into which vast numbers fell and from which they could not escape.

Towards the end of the last century, the south of Scotland suffered from a plague of 'mice' that ate up everything in the fields, inflicting such serious loss to agriculture that a Government Committee was appointed in 1892 to inquire into it, and it was found that the chief culprit was the short-tailed vole. At the peak of such plagues, large numbers of short-eared owls moved into the area, as do other predators, and these remain for a year or two after the numbers have waned. It has been suggested that the enormous increase in the numbers of the voles on these occasions was directly due to the warfare waged by keepers on weasels and owls. Recently, however, it has been realized that these violent fluctuations in numbers are a feature of many species of rodents. The cycle for the short-tailed vole includes a peak every four years.

It was also shown at the Vole Committee of 1893, that the rook destroys great numbers of field voles—

not only adults that chance to cross the fields where the rooks are digging cockchafer grubs, but also the nests and young which the rooks systematically search out.

As with harvest mice and shrews, the short-tailed field vole has alternating periods of feeding, other activities, and sleep, the periods being two to three hours throughout each twenty-four hours, those of the night being slightly longer than those of the day.

The short-tailed vole is absent from Ireland, Isle of Man and the Scillies, as well as most Scottish islands.

The Orkney Vole

Family CRICETIDAE   *Microtus arvalis orcadensis*

As far back as 1805 the Rev. George Barry, in his 'History of the Orkney Islands', mentions a rodent that was known locally as the vole mouse. He says it 'is very often found in marshy grounds that are covered with moss and short heath, in which it makes roads or tracks of about three inches in breadth, and sometimes miles in length, much worn by continual treading, and warped into a thousand different directions.'

Towards the end of the last century Mr J. G. Millais obtained specimens, and on a critical examination found that they differed from known forms in several details, sufficient in his opinion to constitute a new species, which he called *M. orcadensis*.

Later systematists have regarded it as a subspecies, for it was found subsequently that specimens from various islands in the Orkney group showed small differences, but generally speaking, they are much alike, and their habits are practically identical, so far as known at present.

The runs of the Orkney vole are a conspicuous feature of the islands, among the heather and the rough vegetation, running along the surface and at intervals entering tunnels about 57 mm in diameter. Their nesting-places are under small mounds connected by a network of runs. The nest itself is made of grass and roots in a rounded chamber, where at intervals during the spring and summer several litters, varying from three to six, are produced. Before they are three weeks old the voles are capable of independent existence.

The Orkney vole appears to be specially fond of the roots of heath rush, but also feeds on grass and the crops in cultivated fields to which it can gain access. It has many enemies to hold its increase in check, for every bird and beast large enough to capture it, will eat it readily.

Orkney vole

The Long-tailed Field Mouse

Family MURIDAE   *Apodemus sylvaticus*

The long-tailed field mouse, also known as the wood
mouse, is as much an inhabitant of the field, the
hedgerow and the garden as of the wood. It can
bring something approaching despair to the keeper
of the kitchen garden, for its habit of taking the
newly-sown peas (if these have not been rolled in
red lead or soaked in paraffin), digging out bulbs, and
so on. It has also a partiality for strawberries as soon
as they ripen.

The long-tailed field mouse is about 8–9 cm
from the long snout to the base of the tail, the tail
being about the same length. Its weight ranges from
14–25 g. Females are about the same size as males.
The fur on the upper parts is a dark yellow-brown;
the underparts are white. In adults the line of demarcation between upper and lower surfaces is
always distinct. There is a spot of buff or orange on
the chest the development of which, in certain local
races, has caused systematists to recognize four subspecies. It has large and prominent dark eyes—for
it is chiefly of nocturnal habits—and its long oval
ears have the inner margin turned inwards at the
base. The tail is dark brown above, and whitish
below. It is the commonest of the British mammals
in country places, but less frequent in Ireland. It is
common in Europe as far north as Sweden and
Norway.

As a rule it constructs its burrows underground,
or under the roots of trees, and here it stores up
great quantities of acorns, nuts, haws, grain and
smaller seeds for use in winter, when it becomes less
active, though it does not hibernate. It comes in-

doors rarely, and then only in late autumn; its resemblance to the house mouse frequently leads to its being mistaken for that species.

The breeding season begins in March, rises to a peak in July and August, and ends in October or November. Breeding may continue throughout a mild winter. There may be several litters a year. The young per litter vary from two to nine, giving a high rate of increase, which is offset by the inroads in the numbers made by owls, foxes, weasels, stoats, hedgehogs and vipers. The young are weaned at eighteen days, and except for those in late litters, will start to breed the same year.

The long-tailed field mouse is very quick in its movements and when alarmed moves in a zig-zag manner. It will also progress in leaps, looking like a miniature kangaroo, but all four feet touch the ground together although the body is held semi-erect. It will readily climb bushes to obtain berries, leaping to the ground from considerable heights, or if seeking to escape capture, will leap a metre or so up into a twiggy growth and disappear. These mice also swim well when the occasion arises. Accomplished burrowers, they often use unmortared stone walls for runs and stores. They frequently make their homes under stones or concrete blocks half-buried in the ground. They are gentle and apparently timid in the hand.

These mice are gregarious, and the stores of food appear also to be communal. These stores are of the most varied character. They include: leaves of clover and dandelion, with flower-buds of the latter, nuts of all kinds, apples, grapes, gooseberries, crocus and hyacinth bulbs, acorns, rose and bramble seed, slow-worms and eggs. Insects and insect

Long-tailed fieldmouse

larvae, as well as spiders, are also eaten. It has been known to enter beehives, and not only to eat the honeycomb, but actually nest there. A deserted birds' nest is often adapted as a feeding table, when seeking haws in the hedges, or as a permanent habitation, in which case the nest is roofed with moss.

The breeding nest is a globular structure of dry grass, and is usually built in a separate chamber of the underground run, but it may be above ground in a heap of vegetable rubbish. Some of the burrows may extend as much as 90 cm underground.

Little is known of the social behaviour of these mice, except that the female drives the male from the nest as soon as she is pregnant. Also, when two long-tails meet they rear on their hindlegs and box for a few seconds with very rapid movements of the fore-legs, or else they stand and 'sniff noses'.

The Yellow-necked Mouse

Family MURIDAE   *Apodemus flavicollis*

The yellow-necked mouse is distinguished from the long-tailed field mouse by its larger size, the head and body measuring 8·5–12·4 cm, and by the brown spot on the chest (commonly found in the long-tailed field mouse) being extended into an orange cross whose arms are connected with the golden brown coloration of the upper side. It is most common in southern England, becoming rarer to the north. It is not found in Scotland, the Isle of Man or Ireland.

Since there are variations in the amount of yellow or orange on the chest, it is not always easy to tell a long-tail from a yellow-neck and the juveniles of the two species are very much alike. Two marked features will aid identification: yellow-necks are much given to entering houses in autumn, and adults are more robust in appearance, more energetic and better jumpers than long-tails.

Yellow-necks are noisy and troublesome in a house during the winter. They raid the apple stores and bring in nuts from outside, depositing the shells under the floorboards. When scrambling up the cavity walls or racing behind the skirting and under the floor boards, the noise they make is quite considerable.

This species was involved in an astonishing incident in Yugoslavia in August, 1967. A long stream of long-tailed field mice and yellow-necked mice advanced across Bosnia, in Yugoslavia, damaging crops up to an estimated loss of £190,000 and entering farm-houses and buildings. They were so active and aggressive that even the cats would not attack them. The cause of this plague was that the previous winter had been mild, with abundant beech mast and acorns. This increased food supply, and the mild weather, had eliminated the usual high winter mortality, had led to a higher rate of breeding in the following spring and so had caused a population explosion.

The Harvest Mouse

Family MURIDAE   *Micromys minutus*

With the exception of the pygmy shrew the dainty harvest mouse is the smallest of British mammals. It will always be associated with the name of Gilbert White, who first made it known as a British mouse, and its appearance and habits were first published by Pennant in his 'British Zoology' (1768).

The head and body combined measure 50–69 mm, and the nearly naked, scaly tail is almost as long. The thick, soft fur of the upper parts is yellowish-red in colour, and of the underparts white, the two colours being fairly sharply separated. The tail is pliant and the outer end is prehensile, being at once coiled around any suitable object within reach when the mouse ceases to move; it is used as an additional foot when the mouse is moving through grass. A typical attitude for a harvest mouse is to grip two adjacent stems with the hindfeet and wrap the tail around one or both of the stems, leaving the front paws free for holding food. As the harvest mouse only weighs from 4–10 g, it is not surprising that it should be able to sit on an ear of corn. It has bright black eyes, a short blunt nose, and short rounded ears, the latter about one-third the length of the head.

The usual habitats of the harvest mouse are pastures and cornfields, where it climbs the stems of the tall grasses and corn plants, cutting off the ripe ears and carrying them to the ground where it picks out the grain. It may also be found in the tall, rank herbage along ditches or untrimmed hedgerows or even in open fields, salt marshes, reed beds and dykes. During the summer it feeds to some extent on insects, but it will also eat the seeds of a wide variety of grasses. In this same period it stores up much grain in burrows for winter use. Although it winters in burrows in the ground, it does not hibernate. Sometimes it will tunnel into hayricks, and if undisturbed may even bring up a litter or two there. Hayricks, however, are now going out of use in modern agriculture. As a rule it constructs the

Harvest mouse and nest among wheat

wonderful nursery, which has won human admiration ever since White made the species known.

This is a spherical nest, about 7·6 cm in diameter, of woven blades of grass. It has no definite opening, the grass-blades being merely pushed aside to make entrance or exit where required, and closing again by their own elasticity. There is just sufficient room inside for the female and her blind and naked offspring. The male is not allowed to enter. The nest is slung at heights of 6–30 cm above the ground from several stout stems, or it may be lodged between the stem and leaf of a thistle, or a knapweed, or in the branches of a blackthorn bush or broom. The bed is made of split leaves of corn or grass. The nests are not always so tough as that described by White, which 'was so compact and well filled that it would roll across the table without being decomposed, though it contained eight young'.

Breeding is probably from April to September. Several litters of five to nine young are produced in a year. The eyes open at eight days. Excursions from the nest begin at eleven days and juveniles are independent at fifteen days. Until about December the young of the year resemble the house mouse in colour, and may easily be mistaken for it. Then from the hindquarters forward they begin to assume the reddish tint of the adult.

It is usually said that harvest mice are more diurnal than other mice, but some observers have found they have a three-hourly rhythm of feeding and sleep. Though as a rule timid and gentle, the harvest mouse is said at times to become savage and cannibalistic, but this is difficult to believe. It lacks the offensive odour of the house mouse which is one point in favour of it as a pet. Its voice is a low chirp.

Harvest mouse with ear of corn

Harvest mice are said to have decreased greatly in numbers as well as in the area of their distribution during this century. It has been suggested that the use of reaping machines, giving a shorter stubble than the scythe, has been responsible. There was, however, a revival in 1955. There are records of harvest mice in nearly all the counties of England and Wales in the past, and from parts of the Scottish lowlands. Today, they appear to be most abundant in the south of England, becoming more rare as one goes north. They do not occur in Ireland.

The Ship Rat

Family MURIDAE   *Rattus rattus*

The terms 'black rat' and 'brown rat', commonly used to distinguish the two species, tend to cause confusion because the 'black rat' (*Rattus rattus*) is often brown and because black varieties of the 'brown rat' (*R. norvegicus*) also occur. It is now becoming the practice to speak of *R. rattus* as the ship rat (alternatively roof rat or house rat) and *R. norvegicus* as the common rat (alternatively Norway rat or sewer rat). Surveys made of the distribution of the ship rat in 1951, 1956 and 1961, show it to be confined almost exclusively to ports and to a few towns (such as Ware and Slough) which are connected by canal to seaports.

Both ship and common rat are of Asiatic origin, although the ship rat is thought to have been settled here for six centuries before the common rat.

The ship rat is of more slender proportions than the better-known common rat. Its head and body together measures 16·5–24 cm long, while the scaly-ringed and almost hairless tail is up to 25·4 cm long. The weight is variable, up to 200 g. The snout projects far beyond the short lower jaw and the whiskers are long and black. The naked ears, contrasting with the finely haired ears of the common rat, are the best means of identifying the live animal. The feet are pink, with scale-like rings on the undersides of the digits and five pads on the sole. The thumb of the forefeet is reduced to a mere stump. The ship rat is more of a climber than a burrower, and cleaner in its feeding than the common rat.

Although rats have much to do with garbage and

are generally offensive to us in their habits and appearance, they maintain their own cleanliness, spending much of their time cleaning their fur and paws.

In Mediterranean countries and India, where the ship rat lives a more outdoor life, it climbs trees and mostly makes its nest in them. In this country the doe collects quantities of suitable materials such as rags, paper and straw, and constructs a roomy nest, using this for the three to five litters a year. Breeding occurs throughout the year with a peak in summer and, less often, in autumn. Seven is usual, but litters may vary from five to ten. The pink-skinned young are born without fur, sight, or hearing. They become sexually mature at three to four months.

Both ship and common rat are omnivorous; anything that can be digested is eaten. Cannibalism no doubt occurs under unusual conditions, but the idea that the common rat is the more ferocious and has driven out the ship rat by aggression is almost certainly erroneous. The replacement of the ship rat, which prior to the eighteenth century was spread across the British Isles, is largely the result of competition for food and living space. In rural areas, in some parts of the tropics, the two species share the same habitat, and generally in the tropics the ship rat is the more successful and has not been ousted by the common rat except, surprisingly, in some ports.

The ship rat has been divided into three subspecies: *R. rattus rattus*, pure black above, black or dark grey beneath, *R. r. alexandrinus*, brown above grey beneath, and *R. r. frugivorus*, brown above and white or cream beneath. It has been suggested, however, that all are coloured variations of one

Ship rat (commonly called black rat) in granary

species and in Britain all three forms seem to live together and to inter-breed, and all gradations exist between the white- or cream-bellied *frugivorus* and the typical black *rattus*. In London about 70% of ship rats are of the *frugivorus* type and only 3% are positively *alexandrinus*.

The Common Rat

Family MURIDAE   *Rattus norvegicus*

The natural method of dispersal for mammals is that the more adventurous individuals make food-finding excursions beyond the district in which they were born, but climate, mountain ranges, broad

Common rat, also known as brown rat

rivers or seas usually act as checks on further progress. Rats have kept close to man. Where man is, there is food and shelter whether for himself or his domestic animals. When man loads his ships with grain and other foodstuffs, rats have tended to go with them. They even get into bales of merchandise and are conveyed in the holds of ships; or failing that, there are always mooring ropes to serve as bridges from the quay to the vessel. The result has been that, over and above the original natural spread, rats have been carried unwittingly by man to all corners of the globe. The arrival of the common rat in this country was only one small stage in the process.

The origins of the common rat in this country are uncertain. It was thought to have spread across Europe from central Asia, and reached England in ships coming from Norway at about the time the Hanoverian kings ascended the throne of England. Hence its alternative names, Norway or Hanoverian rat. The current theory is that common rats arrived in ships trading with the East between 1728 and 1730. At the same time they were spreading overland across Europe.

The common rat is more heavily built than the ship rat. The combined length of head and body is 203–280 mm, while the thicker, scaly-ringed tail is only equal to, or less than, the length of the body alone. Weight is variable, up to 500 g. The head is proportionately shorter, the ears smaller and covered with fine hairs, and the eyes smaller and more prominent. The fur on the upper parts is grey-brown with a tawny tinge, and is more shaggy than that of the ship rat. On the underparts it is a dirty white. The feet are flesh coloured and the tail is often bi-coloured, paler underneath than above.

The common rat is sexually mature at the age of three months, and thereafter produces three to five litters in a year. Ordinarily these consist of from four to ten blind, deaf and naked young; but much larger litters are on record. They leave the nest at about three weeks of age.

In the country where it is known as the barn rat, its chief enemies are the tawny owl, stoat, weasel, fox and man. The stoat, weasel and fox do not always receive appropriate credit for their services. Admittedly the three also destroy poultry, but there is no question that the damage done by rats is much more serious. Being good swimmers and divers, even ducklings afloat are not safe from them. Rats are equally destructive to property, livestock and stored crops, especially such root crops as sugar beet stored in clumps, in East Anglia. Scores of them will burrow through the cover of earth, damaging the stored roots and fouling more than are eaten. It is in such situations that weasels are most effective as destroyers of rats. Hawks and foxes come into play more in the open countryside, although the rat rarely ventures far from cover of some sort.

The versatility and the destructive power of the common rat lead it to spoil and waste man's food stores and do extensive damage to property. At one time it performed its natural service of scavenger in this country, and still does elsewhere in the world, but as soon as man has learned to attend to this for himself, the rat becomes a mere parasitical nuisance, sufficiently omnivorous for there to be no possibility of starving it out; so a costly war must be waged on a pest already expensive to us. Unfortunately, rat-killing campaigns that do not cover every square metre of the country can only have the effect of temporarily mitigating the pest. The rat's fertility is so great and its recovery so rapid that the loss of nine-tenths of a generation is quickly made good.

The common rat is omnivorous and will eat greenstuff, but it is basically a grain eater, infesting grain stores or wheat and oat fields when the grain is ripening. Although highly successful because it has learned to live so close to man and feeds at his expense, the common rat is cautious of and avoids new objects in its environment. This makes it trap-shy. It is also bait-shy. When it has had a sub-lethal dose of poison it may remain bait-shy for up to six months.

From time to time one hears tell of somebody who has encountered a column of rats migrating more or less in formation. Little is known about these mass movements of rodents, largely because they are always seen by untrained observers, whose accounts are not strong on the details.

In one form or other the common rat has extended to nearly every part of the British Isles and their islets. The white rat is the domesticated albino of the common rat.

The House Mouse

Family MURIDAE   *Mus musculus*

Although it is often found in woods and fields, for the most part this rodent is seen in the immediate neighbourhood of buildings, especially where there are stored foods. There are even colonies of mice in the large meat refrigerators, in perpetual darkness and at temperatures below freezing. They feed solely on meat. They are larger and heavier, have longer coats than usual, and make their nests in the carcasses of beef or mutton.

The house mouse is thought to have originated in Asia, whence it has spread to every inhabited part of the world. Its early spread was largely unaided, but in more recent centuries it has been by ship. Today stowaways go by air as well.

The head and body measure 70–92 mm and the tapering, flexible, and sparsely haired, scale-ringed tail is about the same. The weight ranges from 10–41 g. The snout is pointed, the bright eyes are black, the large, sensitive brownish ears are nearly half the length of the head, and the soft, brownish-grey fur is only a little paler on the underparts. Its voice is a well-known squeak. Although the eye of a mouse is usually described as 'beady', implying keen sight, tests have shown that mice are very short-sighted. The ears, on the other hand, are highly sensitive to vibrations in the air. Recently, it has been discovered that mice use ultrasonics, probably as a means of communicating with each other or even as a form of echo-location for finding their way about in the dark.

The house mouse is chiefly but not wholly nocturnal, active and silent in its movements, emerging from a tiny hole in floorboard or skirting and gliding without sound over the floor, ascending with ease table-legs or walls, and then, if alarmed, taking a relatively prodigious leap back to its hole. It can squeeze through holes as small as 9 mm in diameter and its climbing abilities, also, are considerable.

House mouse

Concrete floors will not suffice to keep it out of a house, for it will climb the outer walls and enter the upper windows, thence making its way unnoticed to the lower floors behind woodwork or plastered walls, till it reaches the kitchen, the larder or the storeroom. Though its natural food is grain, it will eat practically anything edible, and it can exist with little water.

Breeding is fairly continuous throughout the year. The number of litters in a year, and the number of young in a litter, vary with habitat. Mice living in dwelling houses average just over five litters a year, with some five young to a litter. In the cold stores there are six litters a year with six young in a litter. In grain stores they average eight to ten litters a year. The young are born blind and naked, and are weaned at eighteen days. At the age of six weeks they begin to breed.

The house mouse exhibits a considerable range of variation in colour, both darker and lighter than the typical 'mouse colour' and many of these variations may be the result of an attempt to breed 'fancy' mice. One example of this is the familiar white mouse, an albino with pure white fur, pink eyes, feet and tail. There are also dark, nearly black and spotted variations. Several cases of mice that are hairless, except for a few whiskers, have been recorded.

The Coypu or Nutria

Family CAPROMYIDAE   *Myocaster coypus*

Coypus are natives of South America; their alternative name, nutria, is Spanish for otter. They were trapped extensively for the unusually fine fur on their underparts. The coypu is one of the largest rodents, being 99 cm long, of which nearly half is tail, and weighing up to 9 kg. The superficial rat-like appearance is given by the stout body, squarish muzzle and scaly tail. The hindfeet are webbed.

The farming of coypus in Britain started during the 1930s and animals soon began to escape and colonize rivers and marshes, especially in East Anglia where they lived on water plants. Soon after, they began making burrows in the banks of rivers and drains and attacking agricultural crops. In 1962 an official campaign to exterminate the coypu began and now coypus are more widely distributed.

Coypus are active at dusk and dawn. Breeding

Coypu

occurs throughout the year. Each female has about two litters of two to nine young annually. These are born in nests of reeds above ground level. They are furred with eyes open at birth and they move around a few hours later.

The Red Deer

Family CERVIDAE   *Cervus elaphus*

Indigenous red deer are now mainly confined to the Scottish Highlands and Islands, the Lake District and Devon (Exmoor, the Quantocks and Brendan Hills) but feral red deer, from introduction or escapes from park herds, are present from the south-west counties eastwards to Sussex, and also in Norfolk, North Staffordshire, Cheshire, Lancashire, West Yorkshire and Durham, as well as the Scottish Lowlands and Co. Donegal and Co. Wicklow in Eire. Outside Britain red deer range across Europe and Asia, as far south as the southern slopes of the Himalayas.

A full-grown stag stands 1·4 m at the shoulders; the hind is somewhat less. The summer coat is reddish-brown, sometimes golden-red, which changes to a brownish-grey in winter by the new growth of grey hairs. On the underparts the colour is white, and a patch of white around the short tail furnishes a 'recognition mark,' common to most of the deer family, which apparently serves in guiding other members of the herd when in flight from a predator. The usual gait is a steady trot, the gallop being used only in moments of alarm, when the tail is held erect exposing fully the white 'signal'.

The true home of the red deer is in dense wood-lands. These deer are browsers rather than grazers,

Red deer stag roaring

and enforced present-day changes in feeding habits have led to a wide variation in both body size and size of antlers. In English woodlands the maximum weight is 190 kg but on Scottish moors, where the feed is poor and mainly grass, it is seldom more than 95 kg.

The function of the antlers is still problematic, but the likelihood is that they are more an indication of social rank than any form of defence. The antlers are used in fights between rival stags, but even then the main force of the encounter is in butting with the forehead.

The antlers are cast between February and April, the young ones casting theirs later than the older stags. The coat is moulted in May. In spring and summer while their antlers are growing the stags live apart, solitarily or in small groups, but in early autumn when new antlers are fully grown, clean and hard, the stag's 'belling' call to the hinds, or challenge to a rival, may be heard. From early September to mid-October the stags visit increasingly the peat bogs and muddy pools in which to wallow.

There is a good deal of furious fighting when two stags of similar age and strength meet in the vicinity of the hinds. The stag is then in prime condition, his neck and shoulders clothed in a thick mantle of long brown hair, and his head adorned with antlers that reveal his age. It has usually been assumed that the antlers serve to make the stag attractive to the hinds but the hinds seem quite indifferent to the stag's antlers, his rampaging rushes round the harem or to his bellowings. In fact, some observers maintain that certain stags known as hummels, that are without antlers, breed more successfully. The points on the antlers increase in number with age and when twelve are present the stag is known as royal.

The mating of the red deer takes place in the autumn; and in the spring the hinds separate, each retiring to a lonely spot among the bracken where her single calf (rarely two) is born from the end of May to mid-June. A calf is born already covered with fur, and its back and sides are dappled with white after the manner of the fallow deer, but the spots on the red deer are not retained beyond calfhood. The calf is able to stand within a few minutes of birth and can run within a few hours, but it does not feed itself until eight to ten months old and remains with the mother until the following autumn. The hinds are sexually mature at three years of age and bear their first calves at four years.

Red deer are grazers and browsers, feeding on grass and the young shoots of trees and shrubs. In addition to the damage to the plantations of young trees, agricultural land can be harmed badly by them, a whole field of turnips being ruined in a night by a visit from a herd of deer. They also destroy wheat, potatoes and cabbages. Additional natural foods include toadstools, acorns and chestnuts. Seaweed is eaten when the deer are living near the coast. Wild fruits are taken in the autumn. Feeding is mainly at dawn and dusk.

In Britain today the only enemy of adult deer is man, but the calves may be taken by foxes, wild cats and eagles.

Red deer are fairly silent. The hind barks a warning or gives a nasal bleat when alarmed, and the stag uses a gruff bark. The best-known call is the roar of the stag during the rut, a terrifying sound when heard at close quarters, and the hind may occasionally roar in summer. The calf will call, when distressed or alarmed, with a high-pitched bleat or scream.

The Fallow Deer

Family CERVIDAE   *Dama dama*

The fallow deer is readily recognizable by its palmate antlers, flattened and expanded in all the branches of the upper part, though the main stem or 'beam' is rounded as in the red deer. Only the buck wears antlers. The main part of the antler forms a broad, curved plate, the margins of which are drawn out in a number of flat points. Its description 'palmate antler' refers to the resemblance to the palm of the hand with its finger prolongations. The antlers are shed annually in May, and the new antlers are fully grown and clear of velvet by the end of August.

The fallow deer is smaller than the red deer, the buck standing only a little more than 91 cm at the shoulder, and the doe somewhat less. It also differs in colour from the red deer, being a paler red or reddish yellow above spotted with white, with yellowish white on the underparts. The tail is longer than that of the red deer, and is kept in constant motion from side to side. The vertical white stripe on either side of the rump shows up strongly when the animal is in retreat. This is probably an alarm signal, the hairs, being erected, making the stripes show more white, thus flashing the alarm from one to the other through the herd. In winter the fur is a greyish-brown, the change taking place in October. Some of the park herds show this dark coloration at all seasons. It has been suggested that they are descended from a darker, hardier race introduced from Norway by James I; but one authority claims this variety was in Windsor Park as far back as the year 1465. The dark form may be seen in Epping Forest, also in Richmond Park and Bushey Park, where, however, the lighter form is in the majority. The fallow is a native of southern Europe, its range extending along the Mediterranean border and into Asia Minor. It is said to have been introduced into Britain by the Romans, though fossil remains found here suggest that it may have been a true native originally. Nevertheless, not all authorities agree and it is still an open question whether these fossil remains represent the fallow deer.

During its first year the fallow fawn gives no sign of antlers, but in its second it produces a pair of

Fallow buck in velvet

short unbranched prongs, which give the fawn the name of 'pricket'. The next year the simple prongs are succeeded by antlers that bear two forward tines, and the extremity of the beam is slightly expanded and flattened, and its margin indented. In the fourth year the form is similar but more developed, the flat portion of the beam being much larger and its outer margin more regularly toothed or snagged. The fifth year shows further advance along the same lines, and the animal then becomes known as a 'buck of the first head'. In later years the additions are represented merely by an increase in the number of spillers or snags to the flattened beam.

In October the bucks gather the does into harems, and in the course of this there is a certain amount of fighting, but this is mainly show. Throughout the winter fallow deer may be encountered in mixed herds of both sexes. At other times the sexes are segregated, the mixed herds reforming after mid-summer. In winter fallow deer not only browse young shoots but the does more especially kill many small trees by eating their bark. They also eat acorns, chestnuts, and horse-chestnuts. Their main food is, however, grasses and herbs. Feeding is mainly at dawn and dusk although fallow deer may sometimes be seen about in the daytime, particularly in winter, apart from the old bucks which tend to be mainly nocturnal and rarely seen.

The rut lasts about a month, during which time does of two years or older become pregnant. The fawns are born in May or June far in among the bracken. There is mostly only one at a birth, occasionally two, and rarely three. The fawn is able to run within a few hours of birth, but it tends to do this only in emergency. When approached the fawn lies perfectly still until the last moment, when it bounds rapidly away.

Although only the bucks have antlers, it is the does that protect the herd. It is they that alert it and when it moves off we see, as likely as not, when the herd is caught in the open, the massed antlers of the bucks huddled at the centre, surrounded by a screen of does. As the van of the herd draws near to cover, the ranks of the does open and the bucks, with one accord, take the lead in seeking the security of cover. The fallow's preference is, however, to seek security in thick cover rather than in flight.

The name fallow is the Anglo-Saxon *fealewe*, and indicates the fulvous or tawny colour of the lighter race.

The Roe Deer

Family CERVIDAE   *Capreolus capreolus*

The roe is found mostly in open woods. It is the smallest and most dainty of our native species, and appears to have been formerly the most widely distributed of the three, although absent from Wales and Ireland. It would appear to have been driven farther and farther north by the increasing human settlement in the south. As a truly wild animal it had disappeared from England, but there have been a number of reintroductions to forests, in widely separated parts of the country, in sixteen counties. There, although in places very numerous, its ability to move stealthily through dense cover makes the chance of seeing it remote, more particularly as the roe is largely nocturnal in habit, feeding mainly at dusk and dawn. In moderately well-populated areas of southern England some inhabitants often see roe in their gardens in the early morning, but more commonly found are the numerous hoof-marks (slots) in soft ground.

A well-grown roe buck stands about 76 cm at the shoulder and weighs up to 32 kg; the doe being smaller, does not exceed 21 kg. In summer the coat is bright red-brown, short and smooth; but in winter it becomes long and brittle, and the colour changes to a warm grey. The tail is so short as to be scarcely visible among the surrounding hairs which, as well as the underparts and the inner sides of the thighs, are white. The ears are relatively larger than those of the other species, covered with long hairs and whitish inside. The roe has a white chin and a white spot on each side of the dark muzzle.

There are no signs of antlers in first-year fawns; in the second year they make their appearance as simple unbranched prongs. The third year the antlers are forked, a short tine pointing forwards; those of the fourth year have an additional tine directed backwards, and this marks the full extent of their growth. In later years they have the same general design, although they grow larger each year but even at their maximum they are only 20–23 cm long, and are nearly upright. Small though these antlers are, they can be dangerous, if only accidentally, and they have on occasion caused fatal injuries to human beings. They are shed in November to December. The new antlers are fully grown and clear of velvet by April or early May.

Roe deer are monogamous. They never congregate in herds, but form small family groups, which persist until the end of the winter when the young are driven away. In spring the doe retires deep into the covert, where her two, rarely one or

*Young
roe buck*

149

three, fawns are born. They are spotted for the first year only. When they are about a fortnight old, she brings them out into the more open parts to join the buck.

The roe is a good swimmer and often crosses rivers, probably in order to get a change of food, though sometimes there is no apparent reason. They have been known to swim across wide pieces of water, and even arms of the sea.

Leaves are browsed and berries eaten, as well as fungi and clover. Bark is rarely eaten. Foods range from the foliage of broad-leaved trees and shrubs to yew and pine shoots, heather and juniper, as well as briar, bramble and privet.

Outside Britain, the roe extends across Europe, from the Mediterranean in the south to the level of southern Scandinavia in the north, and thence into Asia.

The Sika Deer

Family CERVIDAE _Cervus nippon_

The sika deer is smaller than the red deer, up to 90 cm at shoulder, 63 kg weight, buff-brown with faint spots in summer, greyish brown in winter, the head always greyer than the flanks. The rump is white bordered with black. The tail is short, usually white. The antlers are similar to those of the red deer but simpler.

Sika live in open woodland, mainly solitarily or in small groups. Even at the rut, in late September or early October, there are only groups of half a dozen hinds, each with its stag. Hinds and stag give a sharp scream when alarmed and during the rut the

Sika deer

stag sometimes gives a whistle, rising and falling and ending in a grunt.

This deer was introduced from Japan in the mid-nineteenth century but frequent escapes from parks, especially during the two world wars, have led to the sika being feral in numerous counties in England and Scotland. It is particularly likely to be seen in southern England, from Kent to Devon, and in north-east England.

The Muntjac

Family CERVIDAE   *Muntiacus reevesi*

A small feral deer, not more than 42 cm at the
shoulder and weighing at most 22 kg, the muntjac is
also known as the barking or rib-faced deer. It barks
like a dog and is called rib-faced because of long
dark slit-openings of prominent scent glands that
run down on either side of the face. Muntjac keep
close to dense undergrowth and being extremely shy
are seldom seen. The males have short, two-tined
antlers, borne on long bony, skin-covered pedicles,
and tusk-like canine teeth. The coat is reddish.

Two species, the Indian muntjac *M. muntjac* and
the Chinese muntjac *M. reevesi* have been introduced, the first in 1890, the second in 1900, but it is
the second species that has become established,
particularly in the home counties and East Anglia.

The Chinese Water Deer

Family CERVIDAE   *Hydropotes inermis*

This deer is larger than the muntjac and has a light
reddish-brown coat in summer stippled with black.
Its winter coat is dark brown. The male has no
antlers but it has tusk-like canines, used with a sideways slashing blow in defence. The head and ears
are buff with white round the eyes, nose, and chin,
and inside the ears.

The Chinese water deer lives among long grass or
in undergrowth and scuttles away like a rabbit when
disturbed. During the rut, in December, the male
whistles, and the alarm call at all times is a scream.
The doe has four to five fawns in May–June, some-

times six to seven, and she has four teats instead of the usual two of deer.

The deer was introduced at Woburn, in Bedford-shire in 1900, and has since escaped and spread into neighbouring counties. It is known to be in counties as far away as Hampshire and Shropshire, and may be elsewhere also but, like the muntjac, does not readily show itself and so tends to pass unnoticed.

Chinese water deer

The Slow-worm

Family ANGUIDAE   *Anguis fragilis*

The snake-like slow-worm, alternatively known as the blind-worm, or dead-adder, is a legless lizard. Internally, there are vestiges of the shoulder- and hip-girdles, evidence that its ancestors moved on four legs. A slow-worm also has eyelids like other lizards, the two halves of the lower jaw are joined in front, another characteristic of the lizards, and its tongue is notched, not forked like that of a snake.

The slow-worm may attain a maximum length of 43–46 cm, but the average 'large' example is about 30 cm long. The head is small and short, not so broad as the body just behind it. The tail, which is much longer than the head and body, and longer in the male than in the female, tapers gradually to end in a sharp point. Often the tapering is absent, because the tail has been thrown off. Slow-worms part more readily with the tail than either of our other two lizards, but the new tail is never as perfect as the part it replaces. There is usually a ragged end to the old part, and the narrower new part appears as if clumsily thrust inside the fringe of old scales.

The scales covering both upper and lower sides of the body are nearly uniform in size and shape, broader than in the other lizards and rounded on the hind margin which is thinner than the dark-coloured central part of the scale. Handling a live slow-worm gives a clear idea of its smoothness and the close attachment of its scaly covering. It feels, in fact, as if it has no scales. A thin dark line down the centre of the back and another on the upper parts of each side usually indicate the female. The mouth is small and the jaws carry teeth uniform in size and slightly curved, so that the points are all directed backwards. The eyes are placed low down on the head. The head regions are not so clearly mapped out as in the other species of lizards.

Though the slow-worm may be found on the edge of the wood, or on the heath, sunning itself early in the spring, and apparently a lifeless casting in bronze, on the slightest alarm it dives into the leaf-litter and speedily disappears. It is at this time that they come into the open for mating and later the pregnant females bask in the sun. Later in the year they are more likely to be seen at dusk, coming out to feed. Slow-worms are regular burrowers, spending much time underground, or lying in the earth with only the head showing. They can swim if necessary.

The food of the slow-worm is governed by the small size of the mouth. Our knowledge of its food preferences has been derived mainly from slow-worms in captivity. It will take spiders, small earthworms, and small insects; but always shows a marked preference for the small greyish-white slug (*Agriolimax agrestis*) that is so great a pest on tender green vegetables. The slow-worm consumes this slug in quantity, but where it is missing they will take others. They will also eat snails, slowly pulling them from their shells as they swallow them. The principal feeding time is soon after sunset, or after rain, when the slugs themselves come out to feed.

Mating takes place from late April to June, the breeding season being marked by a great deal of fighting between the males. The female is ovo-viviparous, the eggs hatching within the body. Litters of six to twelve, but as few as four or as many as nineteen young are born in late August or September. The young are up to 9 cm long, silver or golden in colour with black underparts and a thin black line running down the middle of the back. Very active, they are able to fend for themselves from the moment of birth, catching insects, but showing a marked preference for slugs small enough to pass through their tiny mouths. On rare occasions the eggs are deposited before hatching.

Slow-worms spend the day under flat stones or logs and in burrows. Their principal enemies are the adder and the hedgehog, but they are also taken by birds of prey, smooth snakes, badgers, rats, foxes and poultry. Young slow-worms are particularly vulnerable and their enemies include frogs and toads. In October the slow-worm hibernates in an underground burrow or a hollow beneath a large stone, but it is the first of our reptiles to reappear at the very beginning of spring. As many as twenty may be found in one hibernaculum. Slow-worms cast their skin or cuticle about four times a year but the frequency of the sloughing depends upon whether it is a good slug year or not, for the shedding of the cuticle is in response to the need for more room for the growing body.

Slow-worms have been known to live in captivity for up to thirty years, the record being fifty-four. Sexual maturity is not attained until four to five years of age in the females and three years in the males.

It was in the slow-worm that the discovery was made in 1886 of vestiges of a degenerate median eye connected with the pineal gland. This led to a good deal of investigation which, it was hoped, would reveal the function of this gland and the significance of the third, or pineal, eye, but we are still little wiser on these two points.

Slow-worms

e slow-worm is generally distributed through-out the British Isles with the exception of Ireland; it is much more plentiful in the south and south-west of England than in the east or north, but even in the south it is much more abundant in some districts than in others. In southern England a variety is sometimes seen, known as the blue-spotted slow-worm, with blue spots or stripes, sometimes so closely set that the animal appears blue all over.

The Sand Lizard

Family LACERTIDAE   *Lacerta agilis*

The sand lizard is found only in certain restricted localities in the southern counties of Dorset, Hampshire and Surrey, and the sandhills by the sea in Lancashire and Cheshire. Its southern habitats agree closely with those of the smooth snake. It is not found either in Scotland or Ireland.

The maximum size recorded for an adult male is just over 19 cm long, of which well over half is tail. The maximum for a female is slightly less. The usual colour is grey or light brown above, with three longitudinal series of dark brown or black, ir-regularly shaped spots, each with a white centre, the one series along the mid-line of the back, the other two along the sides. The spots along the back may be edged with white, and they sometimes run together to form a continuous stripe. The flanks of the female are purple-brown, those of the male showing a marked tendency to a green suffusion. There is, however, a fair amount of variation in the colour. The underparts are whitish or cream, with black spots, but sometimes the spots are lacking.

The green of the male becomes more pronounced during the breeding season, when the normally black-dotted cream of the underside may also show some green.

The sand lizard burrows readily in the sand, but it will also use old mouse or vole burrows. It is more timid than the common lizard, less agile and less able to climb. Its main foods are insects and spiders, but it will also take centipedes, woodlice, worms and slugs.

Mating takes place in May and June, after the animals have come out of hibernation, which begins in late September or early October. The female lays her six to thirteen eggs, usually eight, in a shallow pit she digs herself, covered with sand or leaves. The eggs are laid in July, the young hatching in the same month or early in August. The young sand lizards are grey-brown above and whitish below.

Like the common lizard, the sand lizard is very apt to lose its tail, and short-tailed specimens are often seen, the original tail having been shed and another grown.

There are two species of lizards native in the Channel Islands, and strangely only one of these is usually included in lists of British animals because the islands are politically British. But the fauna and flora of the Channel Islands belong to those of the nearest mainland—France—and therefore should not be included among British species unless they occur also in England, Wales, Scotland, or Ireland. The two species referred to are the green lizard (*Lacerta viridis*), with tail equal to three-quarters of its entire length and the wall lizard (*L. muralis*) of variable brown coloration and a tail one and a half times the length of the head and body. The green

Sand lizard on ling, on a Surrey heath

lizard may sometimes be seen in this country as an escaper from captivity. It is a favourite subject with vivaria keepers.

The Common Lizard

Family LACERTIDAE   *Lacerta vivipara*

The movements of the common lizard are so rapid that it is not easy to follow them in detail, and it is even more difficult to catch a lizard for closer examination. It runs with a nimble, gliding motion; the body and tail are scarcely lifted from the ground. The usual mode of progression is to shoot forward horizontally from one tuft of herbage to the next, but they also run easily over the shoots of heather or heath, their long, delicate toes ensuring as safe a landing as that of the squirrel leaping from branch to branch. But whereas the squirrel clings with its claws, the toes of the lizard are merely spread out to cover the gaps between the foliage. They are not used for gripping. The common lizard can also swim well and will readily pursue prey in water. A common habit is to seek a patch of sand fully exposed to the sun and there bask.

The common lizard averages about 12·8 cm in length and the maximum attained by a male is just under 17·9 cm and by a female slightly over 17·9 cm. Although only slightly longer, the females are more heavily built; the male is the more graceful of the two, his tail tapering gradually from the slender body to the very fine tip. Though the tail is in both sexes equal in length to the head and body, that of the female appears shorter owing to its sudden tapering beyond the thick basal portion.

The colour is some tint of brown, varying considerably in different individuals from yellow-grey to purple-brown, as a ground tint, upon which are laid variable dark spots forming more or less broken longitudinal lines. There is sometimes a blackish line or band following the course of the backbone to a little behind the hips, and a dark band along the sides edged with yellow. On the underside the males are orange or red, spotted with black; the females, orange, yellow, or pale greenish, with or without black spots, sometimes with only a few small grey dots. They appear to moult, or 'slough', in patches, though entire sloughs are found occasionally.

Their food is chiefly insects, including flies, beetles, moths, as well as ants and their grubs, but spiders are probably even more readily taken. Small caterpillars are swallowed whole but large ones are chewed, their insides swallowed and the skin rejected.

Mating takes place in April or May with some fighting between the males. The name *vivipara* refers to the fact that the female retains her eggs until they are fully developed and ready to hatch, so that the young are born free from the egg-membrane, or else the membrane is broken in the act of oviposition or immediately after. It is often said that they are deposited anywhere, with no attempt at a nest or concealment, and that the mother shows no interest or concern in her young ones. This appears to be true of those kept in captivity, but in the wild the female digs a shallow pit, preferably well concealed in moist soil, into which she deposits her young, in July or August. These number from five to eight in a litter, exceptionally four or ten, and are 3·75–5·0 cm long. Most of them are bronze-brown but a few are black. The underparts are greyish-brown and often the back and sides are speckled with gold. Within a few hours they begin to feed, hunting for small insects such as aphids and other soft-bodied species. The teeth are very small and conical, and unfitted to deal with hard substances; and as the two halves of the lower jaw are firmly connected there can be no distension of the small mouth to accommodate large prey, as happens with the snakes.

The usual attitude of the common lizard is with the extended tail and greater part of the body resting on the ground, or other support, whilst the head and foreparts are raised on the arms, and the muzzle turned to one side in an attitude that suggests listening. It has been stated that lizards are susceptible to musical sounds, and that they may be attracted from their hiding places by a particular whistle.

One of the characteristics of the lizard is the brittleness of the tail. In catching—or attempting to catch—a lizard, it should be grasped by the shoulders. If the tail be held instead, it will probably come away in the hand, snapping readily at a joint near the base. A tail will grow from the stump if the lizard lives long enough, but it is always a poor, ungraceful affair. Like all British reptiles the common lizard hibernates during the winter.

This species is the furze evvet of the New Forest, and the harriman of Shropshire. In Cheshire it is the swift. In suitable situations—sandhills, fallows, heaths and moors—it may be found all over Great Britain, including the Isle of Man, and in most localities it is common. It is the one true reptile that Ireland possesses, and it appears to occur in all parts of the island, though not in any abundance. Outside Britain it is found across Europe and Asia, except for southern and south-east Asia.

The Grass Snake

Family COLUBRIDAE *Natrix natrix*

Before entering upon a description of the grass snake it would be well to say a few words on the structure of snakes, for in a general way our three species are alike.

Snakes have no breast-bone, shoulder-bone, or collar-bone. The ends of the ribs away from the backbone are free. As a result, when bulky food is taken the ribs can be flattened out to allow the necessary distension of the body. The tooth-bearing bones of the skull are connected loosely and the head can be flattened and widened, so that the mouth can admit prey equal to three times the size of the snake's head, under normal conditions. The teeth all point backwards, which makes it difficult for living prey to struggle forward and escape when once it has been seized. The teeth are not planted in sockets. If they should get broken, they are soon replaced by others which lie in reserve.

The eyes of a snake are always wide open, for there are no movable eyelids to close them, and the eyeball has only slight power of movement under its transparent cover. There is no external ear, no ear-drum, tympanic cavity or Eustachian tube, and the ear-bone is attached to the jaw. It seems that snakes do not hear in the ordinary sense but they do react to noises as a result of vibrations through the ground picked up by the chin and transmitted through the bones of the skull. The tongue is long and forked and is constantly used to ascertain the nature of things by smell, and for this purpose is protruded through a little gap in the front of the upper jaw. The gape of the mouth extends far beyond the eye.

The grass snake is our largest British species, full-grown females averaging 1·2 m in length, the males 30 cm less. The tail accounts for about one-fifth of the total length. In this country there is a record of a female 1·75 m long and larger examples are found in southern Europe. The ground colour is olive-grey, olive-brown or olive-green, and this is uniform to the tip of the tail. Along the back are two rows of small blackish spots, and there is a row of short

Grass snake.

vertical bars along each side. The underside, which is covered with broad plates, is chequered in black or grey, and white, but it is sometimes entirely black. It is of graceful form, the body tapering gently from its middle to the very slender tip of the tail. The long, narrow head, covered with large shields, ends in a blunt snout, with eyes and nostrils at the sides. The rather large eyes have round pupils circled with gold, and a dark brown iris. Just behind the head there are two patches of yellow or orange, pink or white, forming a bright collar which serves to indicate this species at a glance. In large females this collar is sometimes missing. Immediately behind it are two patches of black, often united in the middle line. These and the size, general coloration and distinctive patterning make this harmless species easy to distinguish from the adder.

Apart from the head-shields and the broad plates of the underside, the grass snake is covered with nineteen rows of small, overlapping, lance-shaped scales with a central ridge or keel. These scales are an outgrowth from the skin, and when the snake moults they do not fall off as the hairs of fur-clad animals do, but the entire skin with its scales is usually cast intact. It separates first at the edges of the jaws, and the snake pushes against the ground, stones, or plant stems until the loose skin is behind the head. Then it glides out of the remainder, reversing it in the process. In these discarded sloughs the spectacle-like covering of the eye will be found unbroken.

Although the grass snake may be found frequently near ponds and ditches it is by no means restricted to such places, but may be met with on chalk hills, sandy heaths, open woodlands and other places far removed from water. Its main item of food is frogs, but it will also take toads and newts, and it feeds occasionally on fish, mice and small birds, as well as lizards, voles and birds' eggs. The young snake takes worms, slugs, tadpoles, as well as young newts, frogs and toads. It swims well and often enters the water to obtain its prey. It can also climb well. Although an agile reptile, it may be caught without difficulty where the ground is not too rich in mouse runs or too well covered with furze. The undulations by which it progresses are always horizontal, not vertical. When captured it seldom makes any attempt at biting, though it will hiss freely and also give off a foul smell with a strong odour of garlic. The third line of defence is to feign death. In spite of this a grass snake can soon become tame.

In the autumn the grass snake retires to a shelter under the roots of trees, in banks or hedge-bottom, or under a brushwood pile for its winter's sleep. Usually a number of them assemble in the same hibernaculum, their bodies intertwined. Here they remain until March or April, when the frogs, toads and newts, emerging from a similar retirement, are available for food. During April and May, mating takes place. This is usually preceded by a courtship in which the males seize the females in their jaws, and with their bodies entwined pairing takes place. Some time between June and August the female seeks some convenient mass of fermenting vegetable matter into which to burrow and deposit her eggs. If a heap of fresh stable manure is available she prefers it, the heat hastening incubation. The eggs— which may number a dozen or anything up to four dozen—are equal-ended ovals with a tough, parchment-like shell, and all connected in a string. As soon as they are laid they begin to absorb moisture from their surroundings, and increase in size until they are about 30 mm in length. They hatch in six to ten weeks, according to temperature, and the baby grass snakes measuring 15–19 cm make their way out of the egg by tearing several rents in it with a special egg-tooth projecting from the front of the jaws. This soon becomes loose and drops off after its special function has been performed. The young snake sheds its skin before taking its first meal, and thereafter goes through the same process four or five times in a year.

The grass snake appears to live for at least ten years. The female is about four years old, with a length of 60 cm, before she begins to breed, but the male is sexually mature at three years.

The grass snake is widely distributed over England and Wales, and although it has been recorded in the south-eastern parts of Scotland, these records are not strongly credited. It appears never to have reached Ireland.

The Smooth Snake

Family COLUBRIDAE   *Coronella austriaca*

Although in general appearance similar to the grass snake, the smooth snake in the hand exhibits a sufficient number of differences to make its identification easy. The smoothness which has resulted in its name is at once evident to the touch, and is due to the fact that all its scales lack keels or ridges. There are nineteen longitudinal rows of small scales on the back and sides of both of our non-venomous snakes. In the adder there are twenty-one rows—rarely nineteen or twenty-three. Each one of these scales is

Smooth snake

marked with a tiny pit which appears to coincide with the end of a nerve fibre, so that it would appear that the sense of touch exists in every separate scale.

The smooth snake never attains such a great size as the grass snake, its maximum length being 63 cm for a female, and just over 56 cm for a male. In Britain it rarely exceeds 46 cm. Its head is not so distinctly marked from the body as in the grass snake, and the slender tail is a quarter of the entire length in the male and one-sixth in the female. The ground colour on the upper side is grey, brown, or reddish, with small black, brown, or red spots, which are usually in pairs, or they may form cross-bars which give the snake something of the appearance of an adder to the casual observer. Occasionally, another less distinct longitudinal series of spots runs along the sides. The upper part of the head is mainly brown with a black patch at the back of the head; in young individuals more especially it is blackish throughout. A dark streak runs from the nostrils and through the eye to the angle of the mouth. This streak may be prolonged, even to the tail. On the underside the colouring is some tint of orange, red, brown, grey or black, with or without white spots or dots. The eye has a round pupil like that of the grass snake, and this helps to make it look less sinister than the adder.

This species has been found in the New Forest and other parts of Hampshire, in Dorset, Surrey, Berkshire and Wiltshire. It may be abundant locally, especially where the sand lizard occurs, this being the smooth snake's main prey. The usual habitat includes heaths, stony wastes and wooded hillsides, especially near water into which the snake readily glides when alarmed, to hide itself in the mud at the bottom. It is much given to burrowing and spends a fair proportion of its time underground. Its food consists mainly of lizards, but it also takes young snakes and slow-worms and occasionally mice, voles and shrews. When these are sufficiently large it is said to coil around them in boa-constrictor fashion.

Pairing takes place in spring, soon after emergence from hibernation. As in the case of the slow-worm and the common lizard, the eggs are retained until the young are ready to hatch out, and they are born about the end of August or in September, but cold weather may delay this until October. The litters vary in number from two to fifteen, but usually there are about six to a birth. They are enveloped in a thin membrane which is ruptured immediately it leaves the parent body and the young snakes are then 13–15 cm in length.

Like the grass snake this species emits an objectionable odour when captured, and at first attempts to bite. This phase soon passes and it becomes tamer than our other species, with an air of intelligence the others lack.

The smooth snake is found throughout the greater part of Europe.

The Adder or Viper

Family VIPERIDAE   *Vipera berus*

In contrast to the long, gracefully tapered body of our other two snakes, the adder or viper is short and thick in the body with a short tail. The length of an average male is about 53 cm, the average female being 60 cm. The head is flatter above, and broadens behind the eyes, so that it is quite distinct from the body. Also, the shields on the head are very much smaller than the corresponding plates of the grass snake. The iris of the eye is coppery-red, and the pupil is a vertical ellipse, which usually denotes nocturnal habits, but the adder is active by day as well as by night, and is fond of basking in the sunshine.

There is considerable variation in both the colour and markings of adders and this is one of the few snakes in which male and female are coloured differently. Generally speaking the ground colour is some tint of brown, olive, grey or cream but it may be so dark that the darker markings are scarcely perceptible at first sight. Along the sides there are whitish spots, sometimes reduced to mere dots. Those adders that are cream, dirty-yellow, silvery-grey, pale grey or light olive with jet black markings are usually males. Red, reddish-brown or golden individuals, with the darker red or brown patterns, are females. The throat of the male is black, or whitish with scales spotted or edged with black. In females the yellowish-white chin and throat are sometimes tinged with red. The eyes of the female are smaller than those of the male.

The most characteristic mark is the dark zigzag line down the centre of the back, with a series of spots on either side. This may be broken up into oval spots or its indentations may be filled in to form a continuous stripe. The other characteristic is a pair of dark bars on the head and these may form either a V or an X. The broad shields which cover the lower surface may be grey, brown, bluish, black, or bluish with triangular spots of black, sometimes with white dots along the margins. Below the end of the tail the colour is yellow or orange. Specimens have been recorded almost entirely of a rich black, the excepted portion being the whitish underside of the head and throat.

Adders are usually found in dry places such as sandy heaths, dry moors, the sunny slopes of hills and hedgebanks, bramble clumps, nettle beds, heaps of stones and sunny places in woods. Sometimes, however, they live in heathy and grassy places that are damp or permanently wet. They feed mainly on lizards but also take small mammals such as mice, shrews and voles, young weasels, as well as birds,

Adder. (Note black zig-zag line on back)

slow-worms, frogs, newts and large slugs. The young subsist at first on insects and worms. Adders kill with their poison fangs, striking with a swift thrust of the head. Frogs and newts, however, are often eaten straight away, without being killed first.

The adder retires in autumn to a hollow under dry moss among the heather, under heaps of brushwood or into the discarded and leaf-covered ground nest of birds. It reappears about April, and may then be seen coiled on a sunny bank apparently more concerned to absorb heat than to find food. Adders pair in April or May, and the young (varying from five to twenty) are born in August or September. This species is ovo-viviparous. The eggs are retained until fully developed, and when the young are born they are often coiled up tightly in a thin, transparent membrane, which usually breaks during the process of birth. They measure 15–20 cm at birth, and are immediately capable of an independent existence.

The adder is not so amenable to a life of captivity as our other snakes. It is apt to refuse all food and most captive adders die of starvation. On being captured they are always ready to bite; but in a state of freedom they are not as dangerous as is popularly supposed. They are more concerned with getting under cover than with striking. Accidents from their bites are rare in this country where people go about well shod, so there are very few authenticated cases of death from adder-bite. Where deaths have occurred they have been usually in young children or elderly people. The toes or fingers are most likely to be bitten, for the adder's mouth is not large enough to enable it to bite the larger parts. In case of a bite, the standard first-aid treatment is to apply a ligature above the wound, to prevent the poison spreading but this should be loosened periodically to allow the circulation to continue. Meanwhile, the bite can be sucked although it is doubtful if this is desirable or necessary. Keep the patient quiet and reassured, and get a doctor immediately.

The adder is found in all parts of Britain, but seems to be progressively less common from the Thames northwards. It is not known in Ireland.

The Smooth Newt

Family SALAMANDRIDAE   *Triturus vulgaris*

Newts of which there are three British species, are generally similar to frogs and toads in their mode of life and in having an aquatic tadpole, but they differ from frogs and toads in retaining throughout life the compressed tail. As the structure, development and habits of our three species are much alike, a general description is given here before dealing with each separately.

The body is elongated. The two pairs of legs are almost of the same length, the hinder pair being slightly longer. The hands have four fingers and the feet five toes, as have other amphibians. The skin is without scales and is equipped with sensory cells, in small depressions in the skin, corresponding to the lateral line in fishes, functioning as a mechanism for posture and for detecting vibrations in the water. During the breeding season the skin of the males develops into a high crest or fin along the middle of the back and above and below the tail, and the toes are more or less broadly fringed on each side. These outgrowths are sexual adornments as well as swimming aids, and they are also rich in sensory organs.

Newts are terrestrial outside the breeding season, but return to water to breed.

The skin serves the same function of respiration as in the frog, and a newt is compelled when on land to force air into its lungs by a constant pumping and swallowing action of the mouth and throat.

In the breeding season the male stimulates the female to breeding conditions by displaying his crest and his heightened colours, and also by butting her with his head and lashing with his tail. At the end of the courtship the male emits a spermatophore, a mushroom-shaped gelatinous mass, the head of which is packed with sperm. The spermatophore sinks to the bottom and the female takes it into her cloaca. The eggs are, therefore, fertilized internally. They are laid singly on leaves of water plants, each leaf being folded over by the female to enclose the egg. The eggs hatch in about three weeks, the larvae being more slender and fish-like than frog tadpoles. They have three pairs of external gills, and soon after hatching they develop two pairs of thread-like organs from the sides of the upper jaw, which enable them to cling to water plants. Development is more prolonged than in the frogs and toads, but is mostly complete at the end of summer before hibernation begins. The young newts then crawl out of the water and seek shelter under stones.

Newts can regenerate lost or damaged limbs, the young being capable of doing so more readily than the adults.

The smooth newt, common newt, spotted newt, eft, or evat is the best known of our three species. It is widespread throughout England, widespread but uncommon in Wales, sparsely distributed in Scotland and Ireland. It is very much smaller than the

Smooth newt (male)

crested newt, its maximum length being 10·1 cm. It varies in colour, but the prevailing tint is olive brown with darker spots over the upper side, and dark streaks on the head. The underside is orange or vermilion with round black spots, the colours becoming more intense in the breeding season; the throat is white or yellow, mostly dotted with black. The underside of the female is, as a rule, much paler than that of the male, and often unspotted. The eye has a golden iris. The female has shorter fingers and toes than the male. At the breeding season the male develops a continuous crest, running from the top of the head to the end of the tail, and the lower edge of the tail has a spotted blue band with black base. The upper edge of the crest is festooned instead of being serrated.

The breeding habits of the smooth newt are much the same as those of the crested newt. The larva, light green or brownish above, is spotted with yellow along the sides and tail; the tail ends in a threadlike tip. Its change to the adult, which includes breathing by lungs instead of gills, is completed in fifteen to seventeen weeks.

Sometimes, however, tadpoles fail to mature before the end of summer and they remain in the water until the following spring.

After the breeding season, in July, adults and young leave the water and seek their food at night among the vegetation on land. For the rest of the summer, and in the autumn and winter, they hide under stones or logs, in cracks in the earth or in dense grass litter. They become duller in colour, and the skin becomes more opaque with a fine velvety surface.

The Crested Newt

Family SALAMANDRIDAE   *Triturus cristatus*

The crested newt, warty newt or great newt, our
largest newt, attains a maximum length of 15 cm, of
which 6·4 cm are tail. The skin on the upper parts is
dark or blackish-brown and is covered with small
warts. Along the lower flanks is a sprinkling of white
dots, and the underside is coloured yellow or
orange, boldly spotted or blotched with black.
There is a strong collar-like fold at the base of the
throat. The male's nuptial crest starts from the
head as a low frill, but between the shoulders and
the thighs becomes high with its edge deeply
notched, the resulting 'teeth' waving freely in the
water. Behind the thighs there is a gap, and then the
crest rises again as a tail fin, the lower edge of the tail
having a similar extension of skin. After the breeding
season the crest is absorbed, leaving only a low
ridge. Along the sides of the tail proper runs a
bluish-white, silvery stripe. The eye has a golden-
yellow iris. The female, is larger than the male and
similar in colour except that the lower edge of her
tail is yellow or orange. Above the spine runs a
depressed line, which is coloured yellow in the
breeding season.

Crested newts usually hibernate on land, in
cracks in the ground, under stones or logs or in
dense grass litter. In early March they return to the
water. Egg-laying begins in early April, each female
laying 200–300 eggs. This may continue until the
middle of July, when the adults return to land. Some
delay their departure from the water until August.
The newly hatched, semi-transparent larvae are
yellowish-green, with two black stripes along the

back which, later, when the ground colour changes to olive, become broken up into spots, and the flanks and underside become tinged with gold. They have a finer equipment of branchial plumes than the frog tadpoles, and their form is more graceful and not 'big headed'. They also breathe through the skin of the whole body. Some individuals do not complete their development before winter, and remain in the pond until the spring. Their food consists of any small aquatic life such as insects, worms, crustaceans, frog-spawn and tadpoles. On land they feed upon worms, slugs, snails and insects.

The adults, if they did not leave the water immediately after the breeding season, may come on land in the autumn, assembling in numbers in a damp hole, where they twist and intertwine into a ball, apparently to prevent loss of moisture. In this way they pass the winter in a more or less torpid condition. Alternatively, they may pass the winter in the water.

Newts shed their skin much in the same manner as a snake, separation beginning at the lips, and by the help of the hands and wrigglings of the body the skin is worked back over the tail. These sloughs may be found floating entire in the water looking like newt-ghosts; but on land they may be got rid of piecemeal, the old skin being sometimes swallowed as in the toad.

The crested newt is widely but locally distributed over England, but is less plentiful in the west. It is present in Wales and Scotland, but in both there are large areas in which it does not occur. It is absent from Ireland. It is also the largest European newt.

Crested newt (male)

The Palmate Newt

Family SALAMANDRIDAE   *Triturus helveticus*

In general appearance the palmate newt is similar to
the smooth newt, and is as smooth as that species.
There is no doubt that it is commonly mistaken for
it, for a few years ago it was considered rare, but
closer examination shows that whereas it is local in
the south-east of England, it is more plentiful than
the smooth newt in the west.

It is smaller than the smooth newt, its length
being 7·6 cm only. In the breeding season its
distinctness is evident, for the male has then a
nearly four-sided body owing to the development of
a ridge of skin along each side of the back. The crest,
instead of being high in front and having an undulat-
ing edge, rises gradually from the head, is of less
height than in the other two species and has a

Palmate newt

straight non-convoluted margin. The tail appears as though the tip had been cut off and the attempt to renew it had resulted only in the development of a short thread from the centre of the cut portion. But what gives the species its name is a black web which connects the toes of the hindfoot in the male during the breeding season. The tail develops a fin along its lower edge in both sexes, and this in the male is edged with blue and in the female with orange. Another point of distinction lies in the colour of the throat. Instead of the black-dotted white or yellow of the smooth newt, the throat of the palmate newt is flesh-coloured without dots. Above, the colour is olive-brown with darker spots; the underparts are orange bordered by pale yellow, with or without black spots.

The tadpoles resemble those of the smooth newt, and the number of eggs laid by the female may be from 300–400. After the breeding season, the webbing of the feet of the male becomes reduced to a margin along each toe and no longer constitutes a palm; but the truncated tail remains as a specific distinction, though the thread-like prolongation becomes very much shorter, and is the same length as that of the female.

The palmate newt lives more on high ground, although it may occur at sea-level, often in company with the two other newts. At the lower altitudes it leaves the water at the end of the breeding season, but on higher ground it does not forsake the water for long periods at any time of the year. It occurs on the higher ground in Great Britain, so that it is absent over a wide area of the east Midlands and East Anglia. It is not recorded in Ireland, and outside Britain its range includes only western Europe.

The Common Frog

Family RANIDAE   *Rana temporaria*

The common frog is extremely variable in colour.
The ground colour of the upper parts may be grey,
olive, yellow, brown, orange or red, and this may be
speckled, spotted or marbled with brown, red or
black. There are, however, certain markings con-
sistently present: the dark cross-bars on the hindlegs, the dark streak on the forearm, the dark streak
in front of the eye and a patch of brown behind each
eye. The underparts are dirty-white to pale yellow
in the males, yellow to orange in the females, in both
speckled with grey or brown, or, in the females only,
with orange or red. There is a marked tendency for
the colour to change from light to dark according to
the surroundings, the pigment cells of the skin being
able to expand and contract under the influence of
varying intensities of light reflected from the
surroundings.

The frog's forelimbs are short compared with the
hind pair, and the four moderate-sized fingers are
without webs. The bones of the hindlimbs are
unusually lengthened, and this is especially true of
those of the ankle, giving the legs the appearance of
having a supplementary joint. The hindleg is in fact
one and a half times the length of head and body. The
hindfoot has five long toes connected for half their
length by a web of skin which constitutes a very
efficient paddle when the frog is in the water. The
horizontal gape of the mouth extends back beyond
the eye. The prominent eyes are perched up on the
forehead, and each has a fine golden iris, speckled
with brown, and a horizontal pupil. A large circular
depression behind and below the eye is the site of

Common frog

the ear-drum. The skin is smooth with numerous small, smooth warts, especially on the flanks. These are minute mucous glands which keep the skin moist. Slightly larger glands form a pale line running back from the eye on either side. In the breeding season the skin of the male becomes more slimy and the warts on the skin of the female become larger and then tend to be pearly white.

Frogs differ from snakes but resemble lizards in

having eyelids. Like birds, they have an additional lid, the nictitating membrane. There is a row of delicate teeth along the upper jaw, but none on the lower jaw and there are others on the palate. The deeply notched tongue is attached by its base to the front part of the mouth, the tip far in towards the throat. In use, it is suddenly turned over and projected forwards so that for almost its whole length it is beyond the muzzle. It is always stated that the tongue is sticky, but high-speed photography shows that the ends of the tongue whip round the prey, giving a temporary grip, and this must be assisted by the granular surface of the tongue.

The frog has no neck, the base of the skull lying close to the collar-bones, and there are only a few pairs of very short ribs. Being without the framework of ribs and associated muscles found in most air-breathing vertebrates, it fills its lungs by forcing air down with a pumping action of the throat. The skin plays an important part in the oxygenation of the blood. It has been shown that a frog experimentally deprived of its lungs can breathe for a long period through the skin alone.

The female is stouter than the male, relatively longer in the body and shorter in the leg. A distinguishing feature of the male is a pad on the first finger which in the breeding season becomes large, black and roughened, and assists him to hold his mate.

The spawning period extends from February 8th to nearly the end of March, varying with the season and locality. Frogs usually spawn in shallow water, but spawn may be found in water 1 m or more deep. The ponds may be small or large, the same ones being visited each year while others are never used.

It has been suggested that the frog is guided to the breeding pond by the scent from the alga upon which the tadpoles feed, but recent theories assume that the frogs make their way to the pond by celestial navigation, using the sun by day and the stars by night, like migrating birds. It is not certain what brings the frogs out of hibernation.

The common frog croaks only at the breeding season, although occasional croaks may be heard in autumn, just before hibernation. A male will also grunt when grasped by another male. It is a means of sex recognition. Another, infrequent sound made is a scream, uttered with the mouth open, when a frog is chased or caught by a grass snake.

Each female lays 1000–2000 eggs deposited in a mass at the bottom of the water, and at first they are only about 2·5 mm in diameter, but the gelatinous covering absorbs so much water that they swell up to 8 mm, become buoyant and float at the surface. Each of the little jelly-spheres has a black centre—the egg proper—with a white spot on the lower side. In about four weeks' time the black specks will have developed into brown larvae or tadpoles, and having escaped from the egg these will be clinging to the remains of the jelly mass by means of a pair of suckers on the underside of the head. At this stage the larvae have no indications of limbs and their head, body and tail, like those of a fish, merge one into another. Even the gills are not yet developed, though what may be termed the buds of them are seen on the bars separating the slits behind the head on each side. These buds soon expand into gill-plumes through which the blood circulates, taking up oxygen from the water that passes between them. There is as yet no mouth, but this soon appears and horny plates on its jaws enable the tadpole to crop soft vegetable matter, upon which it subsists chiefly. Later on, the gill-plumes are hidden by a fold of skin which grows over them.

Ultimately, the limbs appear. Though all four develop simultaneously, the hind pair are visible first, because the forelimbs are at first hidden by the flap which grew over the gills. As the gill-plumes disappear lungs are developed and the animal changes from a fish-like water-breather to an air-breather, in preparation for a life on land. When all the legs are well grown the form of the tadpole has changed to that of a frog, except for a long tail. This is later absorbed, not shed, and finally the hind end of the body is rounded off and there is nothing left to indicate that it once ended in a tail. The complete metamorphosis takes about ten weeks, and at the end of May or beginning of June the young frogs are ready to leave the water, although in mountain regions there may be some overwintering of tadpoles.

When the change is complete the young frogs, their legs sufficiently firm to enable them to indulge in hopping exercises, still venture no farther than the very shallow water at the margin of the pond, where they can walk partially submerged. Then comes a heavy rain storm and all have the impulse to leave the pond for the wet grass. At such times the ground may be littered with tiny frogs.

At the time the young frogs disperse they measure 13 mm or so and by the time they go into hibernation they are still less than 25 mm in length. By the following autumn they will have doubled this length.

The common frog eats insects, slugs and worms. It has numerous enemies but its chief enemy is the grass snake.

Hibernation begins in October or November. On mild days, frogs may leave their winter quarters for a brief spell, if they have hibernated on land. Many spend the winter in the mud at the bottom of a pond, but others find shelter in holes in banks or in crevices in rocks.

The common frog is distributed widely all over Britain; in Ireland where it was introduced early in the eighteenth century, it occurs now in certain parts only. It is absent also from some Scottish islands. Although still called 'common', this frog is becoming rare. It has been much collected for dissection in biology classes and this, with the filling in of ponds and the use of insecticides, has caused a marked reduction in the number of frogs.

Female edible frog

The Edible Frog

Family RANIDAE   *Rana esculenta*

Although the common frog is the only species native
in Britain two Continental species, the edible frog
and the marsh frog, have been introduced into the
eastern and southern counties of England. In the
early part of the nineteenth century about 1500
specimens of edible frog from France and Belgium
were turned loose in the Fens, where, however, they
are no longer plentiful, though they occur locally in
various parts of Norfolk. Fresh importations from
the Continent have been liberated at various times in
Hampshire, Surrey, Oxfordshire and Bedfordshire.

The edible frog reaches a rather larger size than
the common frog. It is usually without the dark
patch extending from the eye to the shoulder, and
the markings of the body, especially the bright
yellow and black marblings of the hinder parts, are
darker and bolder. Fully grown examples measure
6·4–10 cm, head and body; the females are larger
than the males. The head is more slender than in the
common frog, and the brown ear-drum is two-
thirds of the diameter of the eye. The teeth on the
palate form two oblique lines, and there is a pair of
glandular folds behind the eye. The ground colour
of the upper part ranges from dull brown through
olive to bright green, with dark brown or blackish
spots on the back and larger patches of similar tint
on the limbs. There is usually a line, running down
the middle of the back from the muzzle to the hinder
extremity, light green, yellow or brown in colour.
The back of the thigh is always marbled with black
and green or yellow. Though the thigh of the common frog is barred or blotched, it never bears these

additional spots. The colour varies widely, according to the environment. When exposed to sunlight the frog is usually green, but on emergence from hibernation tends to be brown. Also it is much brighter where the vegetation is light than in dark swamps with sombre vegetation.

It is the habit of the edible frog to bask in the sun at the surface of the water and wait until its food comes within range of its extensible tongue. Its food consists of insects, especially beetles caught on land, and worms. It does not leave the water much and seems more active and agile than the common frog, although more timid. The most distinctive feature is restricted to the male. At the hinder angle of the mouth, just below the ear, are external vocal sacs which can be distended with air to the size of large peas, giving him a quaint appearance. The male continues to 'sing' after the breeding season is past, particularly on warm moonlight nights, when a chorus of several hundreds may be heard for over a mile.

Adults hibernate in mud at the bottom of ponds or at the water's edge, the young ones hibernating on land. Emergence from hibernation is in April but mating does not take place until May or June.

The life-history of the edible frog from the egg to the loss of the tadpole tail follows much the same course as that of the common frog. The eggs are smaller but not more numerous. In this country the number does not exceed 2000. They are laid in groups of about 250, not in large masses. The tadpoles leave the eggs after seven to ten days, but do not metamorphose until three to four months later. Fully grown tadpoles are about 63 mm long, of which more than 38 mm is tail. The young frogs do not wander like those of the common frog, but remain in the vicinity of their birthplace. They become sexually mature at two years of age, but reach full size in their fourth and fifth years.

This is the frog of which the hind legs are cooked and eaten. It is found all over Europe and in northern Asia.

The Marsh Frog

Family RANIDAE   *Rana ridibunda*

The marsh frog was first introduced into Britain in 1935, when twelve specimens were liberated in a pond on the edge of the Romney Marshes. Since then, they have penetrated the dykes and canals of the marshes, including the Walland Marsh. It is not certain whether the marsh frog and the edible frog are distinct species or races of a single species.

Marsh frog

The Common Toad

Family BUFONIDAE   *Bufo bufo*

Most people have little difficulty in distinguishing
between a frog and a toad, but the two are sufficiently alike to cause momentary confusion. A toad
has a flatter back than the common frog and the
hindlegs are not so long in proportion to the body,
only slightly exceeding the length of head and body.
The toad seems more solidly built, with broader
head, shorter limbs and a heavier, more grovelling
movement than the vaulting frog. Instead of the
moist and shining, bright-coloured coat of the frog
it has a dry, dull, pimply skin so strongly resembling
the earth that it is frequently passed by as a lifeless
clod. This resemblance to its usual background is
increased by the toad's habit of squatting motionless
for hours. It is too heavy to leap; instead it progresses
by very short jumps on all four feet which give the
impression of being accomplished only by a great
effort. When in search of food it walks. It swims well
and climbs surprisingly well even if its actions
appear laborious.

The colour of the toad varies a good deal according
to the nature of the soil where it lives. It is usually
some tint of brown or grey, but the brown may be
almost red in sand-pits, and in other places it may
be a rich or a dirty brown, light grey, perhaps with
an orange tinge, or it may be a sooty hue which is
almost black. As it is mainly active in the evenings
and at night, any of these tints serve to render it
inconspicuous in a dim light. The eyes are golden or
a coppery-red in colour. The underside is whitish,
the white being qualified always with an admixture

of yellow, brown or red, sometimes spotted with black.

The skin is covered with wrinkles and irregular and conspicuous warts, the largest of which bear central spines or tubercles. These are glands, the largest of which, the parotid, is seen as an elongated, porous swelling behind the eye. When a toad is gripped, or is even in circumstances of alarm without being touched, its glands secrete an acrid and offensive fluid obnoxious to those animals not normally predators. Experience teaches such enemies to leave toads alone. The skin is shed several times in the course of the summer.

Average males measure about 63 mm, and females 25 mm longer. Occasionally much larger examples are met and such monsters are almost certainly females. The male has no vocal sacs, internal or external, so the best he can accomplish is a subdued croak, used when mating. The female is without voice.

The male develops special grasping pads on the palm and three inner fingers, at the pairing time.

After breeding toads wander away from the water, and distribute themselves over fields, hedgerows, woods and gardens, wherever there is an abundance of insect life, for the quantity of food each toad consumes is enormous. It includes beetles, caterpillars, flies, snails, worms, woodlice and ants. It may also take young newts, frogs and toads, young slow-worms and young snakes.

The toad spends the hotter part of the day concealed under the lower foliage of plants or under a stone or log. As many nocturnal insects seek similar situations in the daytime, the toad has no difficulty in finding food even during the day.

A toad has the homing faculty well developed, home being the hollow it has scooped out, the crevice in a rock or the cavity under a root or stone. In the evening it sets out foraging, and may travel some distance, but before morning it is back snugly in its form, where it may be found during the day for many months. A similar sense of locality is shown in the choice of ponds for breeding. The migration to the breeding ponds is more spectacular than that of frogs. In early spring scores of toads may be seen converging upon a particular pond, perhaps passing some other piece of water that looks quite suitable for their purpose. It is very probable that in such cases the toads are making their way back to the identical pond in which they developed, in the way migrant birds will find their way back to build their nests in the copse or hedgerow where they were hatched. There is similar evidence to that given for frogs that toads must use celestial navigation in both migrations and homing. Migrations may begin in early February, but the main stream is not seen until the second half of March or beginning of April, in southern England, and up to the end of April in Scotland.

The small, black eggs of the toad differ from those of the frog in being laid in series of three, or sometimes four, but within a few days they become arranged in a double row embedded in a gelatinous string 2–3 mm in length. As in frogs, the gelatinous coating around the eggs absorbs water and swells to three times its original size. The number of eggs in a string may be 3000–4000, or more. The strings are wound about the stems of water-weeds by the movements of the parents, and the small black larvae hatch out in ten to twelve days. For the first few days

Defence posture of common toad when confronted by a grass snake

they cling to the egg-strings, then hang tail downwards from the undersides of leaves. They go through similar stages to those of the frog tadpole, and become small tailless toads, a little more than 12·5 mm long, in eleven or twelve weeks. It is five or six years before the males reach full size and possibly longer for the females. Toads are long-lived. In captivity, an age of forty years or more has been attained. In old age they frequently succumb to the attacks of flesh-eating flies whose eggs are deposited on the back of the toad, the small maggots hatching from them entering the toad's nostrils. Natural enemies include hedgehogs, stoats, weasels, rats, crows and magpies. Some grass snakes will also eat toads. Sometimes a toad's reaction to the approach of a grass snake is to blow itself up so that the snake is unable to obtain a grip on the toad to swallow it.

The common toad is found all over England, Wales and Scotland; but Ireland appears never to have had it, in spite of the legend that St Patrick banished it with the snakes. Outside Britain it ranges over Europe and much of Asia.

The Natterjack

Family BUFONIDAE   *Bufo calamita*

The natterjack is smaller than the common toad and its legs are not only actually but also proportionately shorter. But the narrow yellow line that runs along the centre of the head and back is its most distinctive

Natterjack toad

feature and has suggested one of its local names—goldenback. Running toad is the name by which it is known in the Fens, and this is a good descriptive name, for owing to the shortness of the hindlimbs the natterjack does not hop. It runs for a short distance, then stops for a little, and runs on again. Moreover, it is a poor swimmer.

The maximum length of head and body is under 76 mm, and there is no marked difference in size between the sexes. In the breeding season the male develops nuptial pads on the first three fingers, and it has a large internal vocal sac whose use causes a great bulging of its bluish throat. The ground colour of the body is greyish or pale yellowish-brown tending to olive, with clouding and distinct spots of a darker brown, reddish, yellowish or greenish hue. The underside is yellowish-white with black or very dark green spots, and the legs are barred with black. The prominent eyes are greenish-yellow, veined with black, and the long porous gland (parotid) behind the eye is smaller than in the common toad. The male, in the breeding season, can also be distinguished by its much stronger forelimbs.

The natterjack breeds later than the common species, the pairing not beginning until the end of March or April and being spread over May and June. In cold summers it may extend to the beginning of August. The natterjack appears to be less tied to a spawning ground than the common toad, and the locality when chosen is advertised by the rattling noise of the males, a loud trilling croak continued for a few seconds at a time, and of sufficient power to be heard a long distance away. The egg-strings are short as compared with those of the common toad, being only 1·3–1·5 m in length. The blackish tadpoles are 25 mm long when fully grown; but their development into tailless toads takes only six to eight weeks, and the young toads are less than 12 mm long when they leave the water, and under 25 mm long by the autumn. In their second year they measure 25–40 mm and when they become mature between the fourth and fifth years they are only 35–50 mm long.

The natterjack feeds on insects and worms, spiders, woodlice, slugs and snails, and though its activities are mainly nocturnal, it may be seen running about in full sunshine. When alarmed, it blows itself up like the common toad or spreads itself out flat on the ground, 'feigning dead'. The secretion from its glands when annoyed is said to smell 'of gunpowder or india-rubber.'

In hibernation the natterjack buries itself 30–60 cm in the ground. It has also been known to climb up steep walls of sand to winter in the nesting burrows of sand martins.

The natterjack can be found in some English localities and also in south-west Ireland, mainly in coastal areas, but it appears to be somewhat migratory, many places where it has been recorded one year failing to yield even a solitary specimen the next year. A census taken a few years ago has shown that the situation is worse than this. The numbers of the natterjack are declining seriously and the toad has disappeared from Wales and south-west and south-east England. It ranges over much of western and central Europe.

CLASSIFIED INDEX

TO ORDERS, FAMILIES, GENERA AND SPECIES
described in this work

ACKNOWLEDGMENTS

The authors and publishers are most grateful for the help given by Photo Researchers in the selection of photographs, and also thank Jane Burton for photographs reproduced on pages 13, 17, 22, 25, 45, 49, 61, 71, 77, 81, 85, 89, 92, 96, 104, 109, 112 (both), 115, 117, 124, 129, 132, 133, 141, 145, 153, 157, 160, 169, 173, 177, 181, 185, 189 and 196; Sdeuard C. Bisserôt for 31, 34, 37, 38, 40, 42, 43, 51, 54, 57, 59, 182, 192 and 197; Julius Behnke for 149; B. N. Douetil for 165; Russ Kinne for 139; Geoffrey Kinns for 127; A. E. Mc. R. Pearce for 151; Photo Researchers for 101; Leonard Lee Rue III for 83; Arne Schmitz for 95; H. W. Silvester for 74; Douglas English for 121; Ernest G. Neal for 67 and 68; Neave Parker for 63 and 137.

INDEX